DANA'S WALK

Dana's Walk

Sera Johnston

~

Dana's Walk

First published in 2012 by
Ecademy Press
48 St Vincent Drive, St Albans, Herts, AL1 5SJ

info@ecademy-press.com
www.ecademy-press.com

Printed and bound by Lightning Source in the UK and USA

Designed by Julie Oakley

Printed on acid-free paper from managed forests. This book is printed on demand, so no copies will be remaindered or pulped.

ISBN 978-1-908746-37-5

To my mum: for not appreciating you as much as I should have done.

Contents

Foreword

CEREBRAL palsy is a movement disorder that is associated with muscle stiffness (spasticity) and delays in motor development. Spasticity can range from mild to severe and can appear to worsen with age and growth, causing muscle contractures and regression of walking and other functional motor skills. There are many treatments for spasticity, including physical therapy and bracing, botox injections and oral medication. Early intervention is very important for children with spastic cerebral palsy. If muscle contractures develop, orthopedic surgery may be necessary. Selective Dorsal Rhizotomy was developed and refined to permanently reduce or eliminate spasticity in some children and adults with spastic cerebral palsy. This surgery does not cure cerebral palsy and demands a monumental commitment from the child and family. Functional outcomes are predicted and based on the child's age and level of disability at the time of surgery, and progress is hallmarked by hills, valleys and plateaus. Patients are expected to participate in a minimum of 4-5 hours of physical therapy each week for strengthening and re-education of posture and gait, as well as a daily stretching and home exercise program. Families are also encouraged to incorporate standing, walking and recreational activities into their child's daily routines. This can be disruptive to families and finding a balance with school, friends and other obligations can be challenging.

In this extraordinary book, Sera Johnston shares the life story of Dana, her 14 year-old daughter who is living with spastic cerebral palsy. Due to her cerebral palsy, Dana found it increasingly difficult to do basic activities such as sitting, standing and walking. But her Mum never gave up hope to make Dana's life better.

Despite previous excellent treatment, Dana developed increasing spasticity in her legs from her cerebral palsy as she grew. She excelled academically at school but her walking ability continually deteriorated. By the time she entered high school, she was mostly in a wheelchair.

In the summer of 2010, Sera heard about a neurosurgical procedure called Selective Dorsal Rhizotomy (SDR) that we offer to children with a specific type of cerebral palsy, i.e. spastic cerebral palsy. She organized multiple fundraising events for Dana's surgery. In August 2011, our team met with Dana and her family at our hospital, St. Louis Children's Hospital in Missouri. Dana and her parents were extremely articulate and well prepared for the surgery and post-surgical rehabilitation protocol. Dana was our 2,192nd patient in total and 88th from the UK.

We believed that Dana would benefit from SDR surgery and could walk indoors unaided and walk outdoors with crutches after the surgery. SDR surgery on Dana was successful, and in eight months, she was able to walk unaided indoors, and she now walks with crutches outdoors.

Sera Johnston is remarkably open about her daughter's cerebral palsy. This book is filled with frank and detailed descriptions of the severe frustrations and great triumphs at different stages during her daughter's development. Her dealings with complicated school and healthcare systems in order to help her daughter are so well illustrated. Her experience with modern treatments for cerebral palsy is accurately explained. She also describes her successful fundraising due to the amazing generosity of her community.

Sera Johnston offers a touching and realistic narrative of how spastic cerebral palsy affects the lives of children and parents. Thanks to Sera and Dana's openness and courage, this unique book will offer assistance and support to children and parents around the world who have to fight daily against spastic cerebral palsy

T.S Park MD
Neurosurgeon-in-Chief
St Louis Children's Hospital

Deanna Walter, MPT
Coordinator
Center for Cerebral Palsy Spasticity

Preface

WITH the impending arrival of Sera and Glen's first child, thoughts turn to imagining who their daughter will resemble and excitedly discussing the future as a new family. Baby furniture sits in the empty nursery and baby clothes fill the wardrobe and chest of drawers. Three days later than the predicted due date, Dana Amelia is born.

The future has turned into a future of uncertainty and fear. The hopes and dreams of new parents are quashed; suddenly they enter a world that is unknown to them that they have no experience of. A divide emerges between mothers – Sera in one world – new mothers in another.

Despite the treatment options that are met with resistance from the medical profession, Sera and Glen are determined to give their daughter the best quality of life. They discover only by chance a treatment that will ultimately change her life.

This is a true story of mother's journey of bringing up a child with a disability, and also a coaching book supporting mothers experiencing a similar journey.

Acknowledgements

THIS book would not be possible without the positive impact St Louis Children's Hospital, Missouri, USA has had on Dana and us as a family. We are forever indebted to Dr Park and his team, Dr Dobbs and his team and the physiotherapists for their skill, professionalism and care we experienced during our stay. Our thanks also extend to all of the other staff of the hospital who have in their own way made a difference to Dana.

I would like to say a big 'thank you' to the staff at The Residence Inn, Downtown, St Louis for their support, all our chats in the foyer – the highs and lows and for making our stay homely and less stressful. To Stephanie for agreeing to be a critic of this book, and for caring.

Thank you to Ann and David, without that conversation on that day Dana would not be where she is today.

A big 'thank you' to three very special ladies who gave us hope and believed in Dana in her toddler and junior years. Kay, Ester and Sarah you are unique and special individuals.

To all my critics who gave up their time and gave honest feedback on this book. I am truly grateful.

To the staff in Esquires Coffee House, Sutton, who allowed me to sit for hours writing this book. For your encouragement and support throughout our fundraising campaign and to this date.

To Jeremy who was there for me and helped me when I felt I could not continue fundraising.

To the generous community who donated their money and time towards Dana's fundraising campaign. To companies who gave us support in their own individual way. Without you all, Dana would not be where she is today.

To the SDR family who, united by their children and as parents, have a bond of support for a lifetime.

To Mindy for supporting and guiding me throughout the writing process.

And finally, to Dana for being a strong individual and never giving up. Your future is now in your hands for you to explore and find the path, which is right for you.

Chapter 1

$\rightarrow\!\!\leftarrow$

Dana arrives in the world

I T is 8pm on a Saturday evening in May and I sit down for dinner. I am sitting here nine months into my pregnancy with my first child, a daughter. The pregnancy has gone well, avoided all the foods and drink that is advised by books. Apart from the mandatory morning sickness and putting on some weight everything is text book. In the background the Eurovision Song Contest is on the television. It is one of those compulsory programmes I watch each year and look forward to seeing the UK entry and the entries from other countries. As I watch the next singer take to the stage, I feel a pop; I knew my waters had broken.

This is it, two days later than predicted; I am going to meet my sweet baby girl, my first-born. I am so looking forward to meeting her; I wonder if she will look like me. With feelings of excitement and nervousness I take a shower, as I want everything to go well and follow textbook procedure. My hospital bag has been packed for weeks now and ready by the front door. Glen, my husband, drives us to the hospital as he has already telephoned ahead advising of our arrival. We make our way in the hospital as directed and when we arrive on the ward there is nobody in sight, only the sounds of screaming women from behind nearly every door. Standing and waiting by the nurses' counter, my thought is to make a quick exit as I can't go through with having a baby. I am scared; it's going to really hurt. Suddenly a midwife appears to greet us and shows us to a room explaining what to expect.

After changing into a hospital gown I am wired up to a heart machine monitor and, just when I start to feel at ease with the midwife, there is a shift change and a new midwife takes over. I feel I have nothing to worry about; after all, this is the most natural thing in the world, women have babies every day. The new midwife is so friendly and talks through what is going to happen. Looking at the birth plan I have prepared, the midwife discusses with me what I have chosen as pain relief. I can hear my baby's heartbeat through the monitor and it's comforting – quite surreal. I was glad my waters had broken, as I had gained three and a half stone in weight, and I had been finding it very difficult to move.

The contractions painfully increase and the midwife advises some helpful suggestions to ease the pain; gas and air being the only pain relief I had. In my room (although painted blandly), it is clean and has what you expect to see in a labour room. An empty cot for newborns stands in the corner and I picture my baby will be in there soon. The television is on but for me it's really for background noise rather than watching. The midwife checks on me regularly and all of a sudden, she notices my baby's heartbeat is erratic, she looks concerned and I start to think there is a problem. Her next action is to page the on call doctor. At this point I really start to panic and my whole body starts shaking in fear. What's wrong? The midwife is assuring me it is all routine, and calms me considerably. I don't understand what is going on. After what seem ages, a doctor arrives and starts to discuss the reading on the monitor with the midwife. I am trying to listen but the contractions are so painful, I just want my baby to come out. Sucking on gas and air is making me feel sick and I just can't take the pain any more. I feel my pain levels hit a point where I just feel numb. Is this what it is like for everyone, is this normal? I had nothing to compare this experience with and the midwife takes my hand and reassures me everything is going to be fine. The doctor calls for a blood reading from the baby's head and starts to explain how he going to do this. He produces a huge metal-like cone, which he explains he will insert into me to get a blood sample from my daughter's head. It looks like a medieval torture instrument and as he inserts it, the pain is excruciating. He has one attempt and fails, and then calls for an anaesthetist to give me an epidural to block the pain. Waiting for the anaesthetist to arrive seems like ages, the pain is still at its highest and the doctor and midwife are still in my room.

The television is on showing an American talk show that seems to distract everyone's attention as the guests on the show are shouting and arguing at each other. Even the doctor seems to be engrossed in this TV circus show. *Can someone please concentrate on me and get my baby out.* The anaesthetist finally arrives and attempts to administer the epidural and fails miserably. He attempts again and fails again. The doctor now realises the urgency and says: "This will determine if the baby is OK or needs to be delivered immediately." He performs the reading with only gas and air as pain relief. At this point I feel so disoriented and numb with pain, and quite frankly I am so scared what the reading will say. The pain is unbearable; I think I am going to pass out. The reading is tested, the results are not good, and my baby has to come out immediately. The panic alarm sounds and I am rushed to theatre for an emergency Caesarean section. Everyone seems to be running in my direction – I have never seen so many health professionals all at once. As I am lying on the trolley in theatre, everyone around me is talking. I have an anaesthetist, a lady who is seated and talking to me. I look at the clock and it is 1am, I am shaking and crying with fear. I am on my own. I look up at the anaesthetist, and into her eyes. "Am I going to die?" I ask her. She puts her hand on my shoulder. "No," she replies and I fall into unconsciousness.

Waking up in the recovery room, I wonder where I am and what has happened – I feel I had an operation but can't remember why. However, I'm sure I have had a baby. The midwife comes and congratulates me on having a baby girl and shows me a picture they have taken of her. Is she really mine, as I do not feel any connection? Wasn't my baby meant to be with me? Instead she is taken to the neonatal unit, as she has hyperviscosity syndrome. Hyperviscosity is where too many red blood cells are in a newborn's body and in my baby's case, an exchange transfusion is required to lower the amount of red blood cells moving around the blood vessels. Blood gases are taken to check oxygen levels.

My baby, Dana Amelia, was born three days later than predicted, on the 10th May weighing 7 lbs 6 oz. As you can imagine all I want to do is to see my baby in person; to hold her, to feel her, to be with her. It is impossible for me to see her as I am confined to bed and have to wait until the doctor says I can move. I am transferred to my own room and left alone, with my thoughts, fears and emotions. Seeing new mums in jubilation with their newly born babies... why wasn't that me? Hearing the crying sounds of new born babies knowing my daughter is not with me is heartbreaking.

Finally, two days of endless torment pass and I am escorted in a wheelchair to see my baby for the first time. The neonatal unit is just across the ward, and with a video intercom for security, it gives me comfort knowing my baby is safe. I enter the neonatal unit and my eyes focus as I try to seek out my baby, amongst the sounds of machines bleeping, staff and new mums talking. A nurse shows me to a room with four incubators with four tiny babies, and amongst these incubators, I see my baby girl for the very first time. Tears start to stream down my face knowing that at last I can finally touch her. She is perfect and beautiful. "Hello, Dana Amelia, mummy is here," I said, staring at her every wriggle and gesture. I was encouraged to hold her, but I am scared as she is wired to some kind of machine, which seems to be monitoring her vital signs. Careful not to disturb the wires the nurse lifts her gently and places her in my arms on a pillow for support. It feels so good to finally hold my daughter and feel the warmth of her body in my arms. The past 24 hours of pain and anguish soon fade into memory; nothing else at this moment matters in the world, except getting my baby well and going home together.

Back in my room, a female doctor I remember from theatre comes in to talk to me about the birth. As she starts talking, I feel myself overcome with emotion and start to cry thinking about what has happened. The doctor explains the importance of why my baby needed to be delivered so quickly, and concludes by saying that because of some loss of oxygen, my baby may be developmentally delayed in the future. What was the doctor saying, I really am not understanding and feel emptiness inside my body. Noticing my reaction, the doctor quickly confirms a brain scan is ordered to determine if there is a problem. As Dana is in the neonatal area, the scan is done without me being present. It is a while before the results come through and the doctor's words go round and round in my head. What if the doctor was right? What do I do? I look at Dana who is sleeping so peacefully and stroke her head reassuring her mummy will make everything OK.

The results of the scan have arrived and the doctor walks in my room to break the news. My heart is pounding; my mind is racing thinking of what she will say. Is it going to be OK, or not? What will I do if there is a problem? My thoughts are interrupted by the doctor's words: "The scan is clear." A great sense of relief and happiness comes over me. It feels like a huge weight has been lifted.

For the next twelve days I visit Dana five, six times a day, getting to know the nurses and other mums well. There is an unspoken level of empathy with the mums, which by a look you know what to say or not say sometimes. I am taught how to bath, feed and change Dana. This in itself is something of an art. Watching the midwives handle her is quite an experience; of course they are confident and can hold a baby in one arm while doing something else with the other hand. I watch my own baby with slight apprehension, as my instinct is just to hold my baby and help. I make small talk with the midwife just to keep myself calm, a tactic I adopt when I feel uneasy. A routine is quickly established throughout the day and night, which becomes familiar. During the night a midwife wakes me for the night feeds as I do not want to miss any. Walking down to the neonatal unit, there is a stillness and emptiness; no one is around, until I enter the unit.

As usual, I sit in the blue chair next to the neonatal cot with the V-pillow, which comforts me and gives me protection from the Caesarean section. During the day the radio plays music, and for a number of days now the song *My Girl* is playing while I am with Dana. As I hear *I got sunshine on a rainy day* I am sitting and cuddling Dana singing the words to *My Girl*. The words are so comforting to me. Dana is my sunshine on a rainy day and this is now my baby's song and always will be.

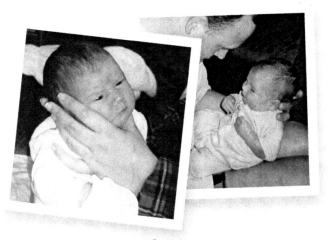

First pictures of Dana Amelia, our baby girl

Nothing can seem to take away the upset of seeing women come on the ward with their newborns and go home while I am still in hospital. The hospital and the staff become familiar and I rapidly get to know which midwives are on duty. I receive a steady flow of visitors that are allowed to visit during set times but all I crave for is the outside world. When I am on my own I sit outside and watch the world go by. It feels so good being in the fresh air, the sun is shining and it's very warm. People passing by smile at me and I smile back exchanging small talk, just to bring a small sense of normality is priceless. As I look around the hospital grounds there is a wall that surrounds the building. Beyond the wall is freedom and home. I start thinking of what it will feel like taking my baby home and visualise pushing her in her pram. *It will not be long now,* I say to myself. My thoughts are soon interrupted by remembering that we are both still in hospital and it is time to change and feed my baby.

Familiar faces greet me in the neonatal unit and I settle into a routine of gathering a bowl, cotton wool, nappy and baby grow. *My Girl* is playing on the radio in the background and doctors and nurses are busy seeing to the tiny premature babies. Once I have finished I sit in the usual blue chair with Dana, treasuring the time I have with her. She soon falls asleep – that's OK – I continue to hold and cuddle her, while watching and talking to the nurses.

During doctors' rounds, one of the doctors confirms Dana is ready for discharge tomorrow and would I like her to sleep with me tonight. "Of course," is my reply. "There is nothing better I would like." Finally, after all these days, I am going to be like the other mums on the ward who have had their own babies with them from birth. Instead of lying in bed and listening to other babies crying, tonight I will have my own baby with me crying. I will be the first person to comfort her, not a nurse. Later that day I wheel my baby from the neonatal unit to my room – my face is beaming as I push the cot. Although feeling nervous at not having the security of the nurses, today is a new beginning. I adopt the same routine as in the neonatal unit when changing and feeding, as it's the only one I know. Trying to comfort Dana during the night without the nurses being first to aid her was frightening, although my instincts as a mother came into play; there is still the little voice inside me questioning if I am doing things right. A midwife comes into my room, presumably hearing the crying and sees I am anxious. My stomach is hurting and I can't seem to get comfortable to pacify my baby. Midwives seem to have a magic touch; they instinctively know what to do. They do, however, make me feel I should know what to do, but at the same time, I am relieved that Dana is comfortable and has stopped crying...at least for the moment.

Relieved that it's now morning, I am excited as I start thinking about being discharged today. Looking at Dana this is the first morning I have woken with her beside me while having breakfast. As you can imagine the feeling I have is beyond words, it feels I am a mum now. I start to pull out a selection of baby outfits from my suitcase, comparing each one for suitability. I have been waiting such a long time for this day and it feels surreal. For weeks I had imagined what today would actually feel like, while playing a picture of my movements. Nothing compares to actually living the real thing. The midwife states I have to be seen by a doctor and a paediatrician has to examine my baby before we are discharged. How I wish the hours away, as all I can think about is walking through my front door at home. Finally, we are both given the all-clear to go home and I can't quite believe that after nearly two weeks in hospital, it has come to an end. Saying goodbye was really more difficult than I had imagined. Saying goodbye to the staff in the neonatal unit was particularly hard. Saying *thank you* didn't seem enough; how do you thank the people who made my little girl well, who jointly used their medical expertise to do what was necessary. How do you say *thank you* for being so attentive and caring, not just for my baby but also for me – guiding me and showing me how to feed and change my baby – for being so patient and for reassuring me.

I am forever grateful. I do make a promise to visit and leave then with a parting *thank you* gift.

My room is clear, and all my belongings are packed. Glen brings the car seat and I place my daughter safely in the seat for the first time. I put a hat on her and wrap her in a soft, white blanket to keep her warm. I look around my room one last time and make a final check I haven't left anything behind. As I walk out of the ward, saying goodbye along the way to the staff, I am so very pleased to be going home. Still sore from the Caesarean section, I hold onto my stomach as I am walking – my walking pace slower than usual. It is such a wonderful feeling to be stepping out of the hospital doors and into the fresh air. I do, however, feel slightly disorientated, which may be due to having being confined to such a limited area. My husband begins the short journey from the hospital on our drive home; as I sit in the back of the car holding my daughter's hand, I am overcome with waves of anxiousness and excitement.

The car turns the corner and I can see our house. We are home at last to a place of safety and a place where we are now a family – the three of us. At the same time I feel scared there are no nurses to call upon for help. What if I don't know what to do? As my mind continues to wander, Glen opens the car door, gently unbuckles the car seat and carries Dana through the front door for the very first time. "Welcome to your home, Dana" I whisper as I follow slowly behind them. It feels so good to be home. Glen and I look at each other. This is it; we are on our own now, the start of being a family and looking forward to a wonderful life.

Chapter 2

⇥⇤

The diagnosis

A few weeks following discharge from hospital, I soon settle into a routine at home with Dana. I am not able to drive for six weeks, so taking Dana for long walks during the day becomes a daily outing. It feels so good being out of hospital pushing Dana in her pram in the sunshine and hearing the birds singing. Once a week I attend a post-natal group where I meet other mums with babies born around the same time as Dana. As you can imagine, life takes on a different perspective and now being part of a mother and baby group, I am thrown into conversations of babies' sleeping and feeding habits. It almost feels like a contest between these little babies; mothers who follow their own methods, while others follow step-by-step instructions from books. Listening to mothers talking is both intriguing and fascinating, and I find myself adding to my experience by listening to what has worked for them. A nursery nurse (who is able to answer questions from the group) facilitates these set-block weekly sessions. As we sit in the same seat each week, it feels as if I have returned to school, as the structure is similar to a lesson.

At the last session a mum from the group suggests we continue to meet weekly at a local hall. I welcome the idea as I am enjoying seeing and talking with the mums. It is such a support knowing there are others who understand and I can share experiences. I imagine the babies growing up together and becoming friends. Conversations during the weeks have the same familiar tone of comparing babies with a friendly banter as the mothers get to know each other. While all the other mothers encourage their babies to explore the soft play area, I decide to take Dana there, too. I notice that there are quite a lot of babies either sitting or crawling as they play. Dana is not doing either, and I have a moment of doubt and start to question why she is not crawling. I become reassured as I notice two other babies who are also not crawling, which makes me believe that some children are simply late developers. This is a well-known fact – all babies catch up eventually.

The waiting room at the baby clinic is full of mothers with babies of varying ages. Some of the babies are with their siblings, and we are called in on a first come first serve basis. The noise level is high for the small space we are sitting in and I'm glad when we finish. I take Dana weekly to check how she is progressing and I find this useful as I can ask questions. Each week I have a red book, which records and tracks Dana's progress. I treat the red book with the respect it deserves as the information, which is noted stems back from time of birth and tracks her progress until one-year old, so it is very special. The health visitors routinely check Dana's development and I mention my concerns from the soft play area. I am reassured not to worry and that somehow gives me permission to relax and put the thought to the back of my mind. Dana will crawl and sit eventually when she is ready to do so.

Sitting at home one Monday morning, Dana (who is approaching ten months) was lying on her play mat and playing with her toys. Hearing the phone ring, I answered the call and was introduced to Dana's health visitor. Having been on a leave of absence, she had called to arrange a home visit, as it was now time for her to get to know all of the babies she is looking after. We arrange a date and time for her visit – and I look forward to meeting her.

Nervously I await the visit from the health visitor and wander around the house making sure the rooms are tidy. I'm not sure why I feel so nervous, as my impression from our conversation on the phone seemed that this visit was routine. I see a lady approach the front door and she introduces herself as the health visitor. Inviting her into my home we exchange small talk and I offer her a tea or coffee. I was not prepared for what came next. As I was chatting about how well Dana was getting on she mentioned the real reason why she has asked for a home visit. She said that there are concerns over Dana's development and there is a delay in achieving the milestones. I do not understand what she is saying and I ask for her to repeat everything to me again. As you can imagine my first thought is a feeling of betrayal, of not being told the truth behind the visit and upset as I am not prepared for what she had to say. I sit with Dana in my arms while a complete stranger is talking about my baby whom she has never met. As I sit listening, I am thinking she is talking about another baby and has made a mistake. Although I desperately want this to be a mistake she refers to "Dana", so this clearly is not an error. Words are said which I do not understand and therefore I am unable to make sense of what exactly is being said to me.

The health visitor recommends Dana be referred to a paediatrician. I remember thinking she has already seen a paediatrician who discharged her from hospital, so why does she need to see someone else. It feels like a whirlwind being swept round and round in my head. I feel shocked, alone with this person in my home; I cannot listen to any more and request she leave my home immediately. A wave of fear comes over me not understanding why a health professional has behaved in this way and also what is wrong with my baby, and why is there a delay in her development? I think back to the soft play area, my instincts were right, although I still convince myself there is nothing wrong. My baby will catch up eventually, as all babies do.

Several weeks pass by before we, as a family, receive an appointment to see a paediatrician. The waiting seems a lot longer and my mind starts to think of what the paediatrician is going to ask or do. I really do not feel comfortable with any of this; I am vulnerable and unprepared for what is to come, while not having any understanding of what to expect.

The appointment day arrives and Glen and I walk to reception and announce our arrival, a feeling of deep hurt starts in my stomach. Looking at Dana as she sleeps in the car seat, she is perfect; there is nothing wrong with her and I know they have made a mistake. We are called in to see the paediatrician and asked to take a seat in a tiny room, which is filled with a desk, chairs, a couch and a child's table with toys. A file with Dana's name is sitting on the desk; why has Dana got a file when there is nothing wrong with her? My thought process is interrupted by questions from the paediatrician about Dana's development, which I answer honestly. The next sentence the paediatrician said to us I am not expecting – "I think your child might have cerebral palsy and I would like for an MRI scan to be done to confirm this." Just like that these few words shook my world. How can she know this by asking us a few questions and playing with Dana for ten minutes? Did she really say my child might have cerebral palsy (CP)? I have so many questions for the paediatrician I can't get my words out quickly enough in between the shock and tears. The answers do not satisfy me as nothing is confirmed; this frustrates me even further as I have no understanding of what this means and feel helpless, and powerless. Walking out of the reception area I feel numb, I can see people sitting in the waiting area looking at me, all I want to do is hide.

A week later we are back to see the same paediatrician as the results of the MRI scan have arrived. Yet again we announce our arrival at reception and the surroundings are familiar with an unpleasant feeling. Sitting again in her tiny room, listening to the paediatrician speaking, my world fell apart again when she said:

"The MRI confirms your child has cerebral palsy." Tears begin to run down my face. My knowledge of CP is only what I had seen on the television. The paediatrician looked at me and said: "Dana has the mild form." What does this mean? Again I do not understand this, as I have nothing to compare with. She explains Dana will be slower and her mobility will be affected. Looking at Dana I can't understand how my perfect baby has CP. I want more information to understand how this will affect Dana, but there is nothing given to me, other than to advise me that Dana will be seen regularly by a physiotherapist.

Dana as a baby sitting patiently

Walking out through reception and tears streaming down my face, people sitting in the waiting area are looking at me. Yet again I want to hide. I have just got into a routine of being a mum, how do I care for a disabled child? I look at Dana, my beautiful baby girl, she doesn't look disabled. How in a matter of half an hour our lives have turned upside down. The paediatrician's words are so cold and unsympathetic. I keep thinking about how we were told; it was very matter of fact. I am angry and upset at the way we are told and the way the paediatrician thinks it's OK to talk to parents in this manner. Glen and I sit in our car, looking at each other and burst into tears. Dana is thirteen months old.

With no information about CP given to us, we arrive home and start searching the internet to gain an understanding. What we read and see are horrific examples. I feel sick and start to cry. This is not going to be my little girl. I make a vow from this day I will do whatever it takes to ensure Dana has the right treatment and care. Deep down I still do not accept that Dana has CP and immediately search for the best private specialist in this field to get a second opinion. There is still a possibility a mistake has been made and an independent second opinion will tell me my baby is fine.

Armed with the MRI scan we arrive at the Harley Street clinic for our appointment and are shown through to one of the consultation rooms. The consultant, a tall man with an air of authority about him, looks at the MRI scan and then examines Dana. He sits back behind his large desk holding on to the MRI scan, looking at us both, pauses and confirms Dana does have CP. Just hearing those words again feels like a rip in my stomach. A wave of emotions starts to run through my body. A sense of loss and grief. A loss of all those early months imagining what Dana will be like running around and playing with her friends. A loss of planning for the future, hopes and dreams thinking back to when I was expecting Dana – how do I know what the future will be like for her. A sense of the unknown for the little girl I have. One thing I am sure of is this is still my little girl who I love dearly, my first-born; I am her mum who will do everything and anything to give her the life she deserves.

I am thrown into a world I have no experience in – a world of disability. Nobody in my family has a disability. Feelings of guilt start to go round in my mind. But how? She is my first-born – I didn't know what to expect – all mothers' experiences are different. If only Dana was born on the predicted date, then things would be different – so many 'if only's. How am I going to tell my family and when is the best time? What will their reaction be?

Dana's signature smile

The family are due to visit on Sunday, and I know that this will be the perfect opportunity to tell them. I don't want to feel it is an announcement, yet it is important enough to ensure the timing is right. The reaction is generally sympathy, with a lot of questions. As I am talking and explaining what we had been told yet at the back of my mind thinking, I am talking about another child, this is not my Dana. I do not accept my child is disabled although my words were saying otherwise. My real feelings are always very well hidden and I start to develop a front for others including family. Deep inside I feel unhappy and lonely but to others appear to take everything in my stride. I want to protect my baby and myself. Little did I know that this is the beginning of depression.

My pregnancy was perfect, although I did gain three and half stone in weight. I had cravings for sausage sandwiches but I also ate a balanced diet. All my pre-natal checks ran smoothly and no concerns were raised. I am desperate to search for an answer, anything to tell me what went wrong. I just want to find a reason. I blame myself for Dana's disability. I am her mum, the person who is supposed to protect. I should have been more demanding. If only I had been, if only…

Physiotherapy

As the paediatrician has suggested, we are to arrange to see the physiotherapist, and given the advice that we have been instructed to follow, then this is the first step. I am told from the first phone call that I make to arrange an appointment, and that the assigned physiotherapist for Dana is on holiday, so we have weeks to wait. This is not what I want to hear. Suddenly a sense of vulnerability comes over me – why is this person on the phone telling me this; does she not know my child has just been diagnosed? I just want my child to see a physiotherapist now and I am no longer interested in Dana's assigned therapist, as she is on holiday. I have so many questions to ask about CP and at this precise moment I feel hopeless at not understanding how this condition will affect Dana. I want to know how as parents we cope with the unknown; what to expect, what to do, and how to care for Dana. My reply to the person on the phone was to arrange another therapist, as I am not prepared to wait for the assigned therapist to return from holiday.

A few weeks pass and a physiotherapist makes the first home visit that consists mainly of assessing Dana and talking through the benefits of physiotherapy. Although the appointment is an hour, I find what the therapist is saying is difficult to follow and the movements she shows me, which will help Dana, seem foreign. This is a different language to what I am familiar with from the post-natal groups and I struggle to understand. Inside I am crying and thinking who will I share my anxieties and questions with, certainly not the mothers from the post-natal group as none of their children have CP. I start to feel alone again, and scared. The therapist visits weekly so at least I have someone to speak to. However, she does not herself have any children with a disability.

Suddenly the realisation of Dana's disability becomes real, although I am still in denial. During the assessment the therapist announces that children with CP generally end up in a wheelchair and Dana will be under the care of the hospital until the age of eighteen. Of course the therapist is talking generally and this was not going to be Dana. Dana was just over one-year-old and she is going to be the exception to the rule. Eighteen years old would be such a long time away and I can't imagine what Dana will be like by then. One thing I am 100% certain of, is that Dana is not going to end up in a wheelchair, and that is very clear in my mind.

Chapter 3

✦ ✦

A diary of appointments

IT soon became apparent that weekly physiotherapy appointments are part of our lives and whatever we have planned for our days, attending physiotherapy will always be a priority. The appointments will take place either at a clinic or the hospital and I settle into another routine. As Dana becomes a toddler, I still attend the original post-natal group. As you can imagine, although the same age as Dana, the children are very mobile, running around and climbing over furniture. Part of me still wants a sense of normality. Looking at these children, who I have known from babies, it saddens me that Dana is not at this stage. I join Dana in the group, lifting her onto the slide and helping her slide down. As Dana slides down, she laughs and produces a smile that makes me forget about the disability. We play together with toy teacups and pretend to drink tea. The other mothers look and make small talk; of course questions are asked, as their knowledge is less than mine. The familiar conversations of friendly banter of previous get-togethers are gone. I feel a clear divide and I feel sad. The mothers and I now have very different children, as I listen to the conversations it becomes clear to me that I can't share my frustrations. I have entered a different world to the one these mums are in and it is frightening not being able to understand what this different world is.

During one of the weekly physiotherapy appointments, the therapist suggests referring Dana to portage, which mainly focuses on fine motor skills. The terminology used is a different language and understanding their purpose takes a while to comprehend. It's clear now Dana is firmly in the system with an assigned physiotherapist and now a portage worker. How many other professionals will be assigned to Dana? The portage worker has a very calming appearance and a playful nature, bonding with Dana instantly. Her home visits are welcomed and always encouraging. She has the ability to lessen my anxieties, and Dana always shows off what she is able to do. I take an instant liking to her as I am able to ask any questions and am not made to feel foolish. During one of the portage appointments a suggestion is made to me for Dana to attend weekly sessions at an intensive therapy centre, especially designed for children with CP. As the portage worker is talking about how this will benefit Dana, I feel a sense of hope for the first time, and knew that there had to be something else to help my daughter. The portage worker offers to come with me for the initial visit.

The therapy room is full of colourful children's artwork and toys in every corner. There is no mistake that this is a room designed for therapy, as plinths (wooden slatted high tables), benches and wooden frames fill the room. The children in Dana's session are of the same age and with very different abilities. At each session I stay with Dana during therapy, which is led by a specialist therapist and assist with the activity – all done through play and nursery rhymes. At the end of each session all the children sit around a table and eat a snack. This also teaches children basic skills of how to hold cutlery and drink from a cup. This is the time I find myself talking with the other mothers. Finally I have mothers with whom I can talk to; who understand. It feels at this moment I am beginning to lead two different lives; one in a disabled world, and one in a non-disabled world.

Although the therapy sessions at the specialist centre are benefitting Dana, the physiotherapy sessions still continue, despite becoming less frequent and shorter. Dana is seen by a range of physiotherapists that result in various different approaches and opinions leading to inconsistency of sessions. New physiotherapists assess Dana on their first visit, which to me always feels that we are starting again from scratch. This frustrates me, as I am repeatedly asked the same questions by different therapists. The physiotherapy sessions consist of stretching exercises and through play, incorporating therapy; for example, catching a ball or reaching up with one hand for a soft toy. The format is always the same for each appointment, stretch Dana's legs, and then some therapy. From a young age when a ball was thrown for Dana to catch, she would always close her eyes; this was no different at the physiotherapy session. Even today, although she doesn't close her eyes, you can see she looks uncomfortable at catching a ball, although she can do it – occasionally.

Dana having fun with her nanny

Being thrown into the world of physiotherapy I am desperate to get a better understanding when particular exercises are done; how this will benefit Dana, and I will always ask lots of questions. My knowledge of exercises is what I know and do at the gym and I have a basic understanding of the muscles used, but I want to understand how these exercises are specifically helping Dana. Sometimes the answers are quite reassuring, while at other times, quite negative. This is the case when I ask if by increasing the amount of physiotherapy, will this make Dana stronger and enable her to walk one day. The response to me is that Dana will never walk and will end up in a wheelchair for the rest of her life. That moment I feel heartbroken. I picture Dana sitting in a wheelchair alone, relying on others for help and feel an ache in my stomach. I'm filled with hope when I ask the question and then squashed when I hear the reply. How does she know Dana will end up in a wheelchair, as I know she will not? Her words and the picture of Dana in the wheelchair keep going around my head, days and weeks after she has seen her. When someone tells me that I can't do something, then being the person that I am, I will find a way to do it. This is no different, I am not sure how and when, but I know one day Dana will walk.

Dana is very much in the 'system' and now has an assigned consultant in addition to the original paediatrician who had seen Dana and gave us the CP diagnosis. The calendar at home is filling up with appointments to see the consultant, physiotherapist, and paediatrician while having to attend weekly specialist therapy. It very much becomes Dana's schedule and time is taken out of nursery to attend these appointments. Each appointment is very separate from each other yet has a familiar routine of answering the same questions, although each appointment has a different focus. The hospital appointment with the consultant is a time to raise any concerns about Dana's CP. Decisions are made, based on how Dana's body is developing as a result of the CP, even with physiotherapist input. At one of these appointments, the consultant suggests for

Dana to have Botox, which, with intensive physiotherapy, can be an effective way of strengthening weaker muscles. Dana has Botox on three separate occasions and on two occasions, and also has a full leg plaster fitted for six weeks to give an extra stretch to the muscle. For Dana, these Botox procedures have not made an overall difference to Dana's spasticity. As a mother, I am guided by the benefits of the treatment as explained to me by the consultant and it is difficult to comprehend a procedure may not benefit your child – my hope is every procedure I agree to will give Dana the maximum benefit and will work.

What is not clear to me at the time of diagnosis is how the CP will affect Dana's body as she grows. Crucially, although CP is not a condition which progressively worseness, it does have an effect on the body.

Orthotics

From the age of two Dana has orthotic splints made, which over time are renewed as her feet grow. Again, these appointments are at the hospital, where a cast of Dana's feet and legs are taken and while this is being done, I distract Dana by helping her choose a colour for her new splints from a folder. The folder is made up of different colours and designs to choose from ranging from baby, toddler and older children's themes. Dana chooses pink with little flowers. The purpose of these splints is to support the feet in the correct position when she walks while also stretching.

During the hospital and physiotherapy appointments it becomes clear Dana's right foot, especially, is turning inwards when walking and the splints will enable the foot to be fixed in the correct position. Although the right foot is affected, recommendations are made that both feet will have splints. The process is very long-winded and can take anything up to two months from the start to finally getting the splints fitting correctly. It is crucial I monitor Dana's feet and as I see her toes nearing the end of the splint, I start the process of making an appointment to see orthotics at the hospital. These appointments are only on a Wednesday, so as you can imagine, they are usually fully booked. The appointments always fill us with anxiety, as Dana has a fear of the plaster cast mould being done. Generally there are tears and screams. The feeling of guilt running through me, seeing Dana in such an upsetting state is unbearable; I try to calm her down. It's not an isolated incident and is the reaction to all orthotic appointments. Dana only calms down when it's finished and I am putting her socks back on.

Dana sitting wearing her splints and standing in her standing frame

As Dana is so young, training shoes are the most suitable type of footwear to fit around the splints. Due to the splints being made of tough plastic, flexibility in the splint is not possible and the size of the training shoes allows for the extra length from the toes to the end of the splint. Measuring Dana's feet is always done with splints on and never as other children's feet are measured.

The term referral is something that becomes familiar as this is used frequently and now I know it means Dana has to see another stranger. A referral is made to an occupational therapist who assesses Dana and advises on any adaptations in the home. For me it reaffirms the disability and the amount of input that is needed, although at times disjointed. The occupational therapist assesses how Dana manages in the bathroom and in the home generally and is in agreement that by providing handle bars, this will assist Dana greatly throughout the home. It may seem selfish to say I do not want my home looking like a home for the disabled; I still want to maintain a sense of normality, although at the same time keeping the needs of Dana as a priority.

The stress of understanding how Dana's condition is affecting her is beginning to show, coupled with the fact I am still in denial about her having a disability. I look forward to the winter months so I can put trousers on Dana to cover her splints. When she was younger and still in the stroller she looked like any other child. I am angry I have to fill her life up with all these different appointments to see all these different strangers, when she is missing out on so much. Joining the 'system' feels like going around a hamster's wheel, attending the same appointments, while going to see one person or another. I feel confined to this wheel and I can't get off. I see the world outside getting on with life and I am stuck.

Finding balance

I aim to maintain a sense of normality during the times when we are not at an appointment. At home one of Dana's favourite children's programmes is the Tweenies and she sings along to the nursery rhymes. Dana and I copy the items that the Tweenies are making on TV. Seeing Dana's face smile and laugh is a joy to watch and her smile melts my heart. Dana sits in a little wooden chair eating a snack while watching the programme, all her toy Tweenies around her on the floor. Her favourite Tweenie is Bella, a strong character who seems the organiser of the group, which is quite ironic as the character is just as headstrong as Dana.

The Tweenies also has an influence on Dana's love of singing and music and I enrol her in a group called Jo Jiggles. The teacher again is very supportive and welcoming. We attend weekly music lessons. Each week the children play a different musical instrument to nursery rhymes. I help Dana by holding her if she is dancing or singing and playing the musical instrument. It is exhausting carrying and dancing with Dana each week, as by this age she is getting heavy, but it is worth seeing the happiness on her face. The most important part is she is again with other children of a similar age and the fact that she is having fun.

An alternative therapy

In the early years having a professional suggest the specialist therapy centre for Dana to attend was the exception to the rule, and I am eternally grateful to this special lady. Little did she know at the time, her suggestion would have a positive ripple effect. It is at this centre I meet another mother who has taken her child to a cerebral therapy centre in Hungary with remarkable results. Although the principles are the same in terms of therapy, it does come at a cost, which is expensive. I research the therapy thoroughly and armed with the information, I discuss this with Dana's health professionals. Nobody is supportive at all. I quickly realise as a parent, I have to trust my judgment based on the information I research against the benefits Dana will gain. Within a matter of months we are on a plane to Hungary.

Chapter 4

→ ←

Budapest – Peto Institute

MEETING and chatting with that mother at the special-ist centre about her experience in Budapest was fate. I could have sat and chatted politely without being interested, but I was very much interested and as I was listening, my feeling was that this would be the next stage for Dana. A therapy where there is a familiar understanding yet needs much longer and more intensive sessions. As I am listening about how the mother's child has improved with the structure adopted by the therapists (conductors) in Budapest, I know this is something that I want for Dana. I am not surprised when the mother said she found out about this therapy from another parent. Why has this been the case I wondered? And now she is passing the information to me. I find this interesting how strangers come together, as they have a common bond – their children. An unspoken word is ample to understand how parents feel; to see parents of disabled children, I have empathy. As parents – especially parents of children with disabilities – we are searching for the things that will improve a child's quality of life. Like the mother I met at the specialist centre – I am no different.

At home I eagerly search the internet for the centre in Budapest and find information on the Peto Institute. An impressive centre;

it was originally founded by Andres Peto in 1945, who was a physician and educator, and who developed his conductive educational system. Conductive education is based on the idea that despite the damage, the nervous system still possesses the capacity to form new neural connections. It is a centre which attracts families of CP children from all over the world and it is a university for students who are training to become conductors, either at the Institute or seeking employment around the world working with CP children. Reading through the information, I print the relevant facts about the therapy to chat through with the UK health professionals. As I was reading, it was clear to me that the conductors worked on specific tasks with the children depending on age and the programme was very intensive. Children generally attend the Institute in a block of four weeks and therapy takes place daily Monday to Friday 9am to 3pm This is a very big jump from what Dana had been used to and for us to consider this, I really need to be sure Dana is able to cope with this intensity. Ultimately, this therapy will work on the patterns of movement through play in a repetitive way, teaching Dana how to functionally move her body.

I send an email to the Institute to enquire on the process and receive details on how to apply, the structure of the programme for Dana's age group and costs. Dana's disability is spastic diplegia cerebral palsy, which means her legs are mainly affected. The muscles are stiff and require daily stretching and she is unable to stand and walk unaided. The physiotherapy currently provided is, when received, weekly for an hour. In addition to this I also help Dana to stretch and provide exercises at home. My ethos is to optimise the opportunity in the early years of Dana's life to make the difference and ensure she has a good quality of life. The thought of Dana when she is older asking me why I did not help her find a treatment that would have changed her life, and knowing that I knew of a therapy which may have helped, is heartbreaking. I will always search to find the right treatment for her wherever in the world that may be.

Dana and Sera in Budapest

I approach the subject of taking Dana to Budapest with all of Dana's health professionals without receiving one positive comment. Now I understood the mother's comments at the specialist centre and how the network of mothers who have disabled children really do come together. I know that I am not going to be supported in my decision to take Dana to Budapest, yet I am not given an alternative by the UK health professionals that match the intensity of what is being offered in Budapest. This is difficult, and for the first time I am acting alone on the information I have, based on factual evidence of children who have had this treatment and speaking with the Institute itself, specifically how Dana will benefit from an intensive block visit.

The positivity I felt had been quashed in a matter of minutes. I feel alone, let down and upset. This intensive therapy is the opportunity for Dana to gain great benefit and improvement. Surely that is a good thing. I have to think what is best for Dana and put forward my suggestions from my perspective about why this is so important. I knew where I stood as far as the UK health professionals are concerned and continue to prepare getting Dana to Budapest.

Dana is two and a half years old as Glen and I prepare to start an intensive four-week programme in Budapest. The flights are booked, the dates are arranged with the Institute, and the accommodation has been found. This is not a holiday and it certainly doesn't feel as if we are preparing to go on one. On the plane I have mixed emotions, of course I am excited to see how this treatment will benefit Dana; however, on the other hand there is a slight doubt. Have I made the right decision taking her to a country I have never been to and allowing her to undergo such an intensive treatment at such a young age? I thought if I have it wrong and do not see the benefit from the therapy, I will take Dana home. On the other hand if I do see the benefit of the therapy, then how wonderful this will be. I had to trust and listen to myself.

Landing in Budapest my feelings of nervousness increase and I look at Dana who is quite happy playing with her Tweenie character. She has brought all four dolls with her on the plane; she has her favourite, Bella, and the others are packed in the case. It's a short drive from the airport to the accommodation and as we pass through the centre of Budapest we get a sense of the city, which is divided by the Danube River – Buda on one side – Pest on the other. The accommodation is essentially built as one and two bedroom apartments with the facility of a large therapy room on the ground floor. Quite a few international families stay here, including from the UK as we discover during our stay. There is a sense of community as the accommodation is linked to the Institute and has a shuttle bus service for the families between the two sites. Families gather in a communal area, which is set up with sofas, TV and games for the children. Families who have been staying for a while welcome us and soon we are chatting and settle in for our time in Budapest. It is interesting to hear from the other parents on why they had decided to come, and although not surprisingly, it is the same reason as mine. Again, this familiar sense of bonding is starting to form, and as we talk, I know exactly how the mothers feel. Their children are older than Dana and I start wondering if Dana will be similar at the same age. If only I had a crystal ball to see into the future. If only...

Today is the day for the first visit at the Peto Institute and Glen and I have an appointment with the head of department who will assess Dana and talk through the programme and what to expect. We have been informed that the shuttle bus leaves at the same time every morning to take the families to the Institute and we must be in reception in good time. Boarding the bus there are more families than I had met when we arrived and all different nationalities. Looking at the children boarding the bus, some much older in age, I think to myself that this will not be Dana, because she was having this therapy at a younger age and would only need a few sessions. However, little did I know then that we would spend the next six years attending the Peto Institute.

As we drive through the city the children who already know each other chat happily while I have Dana sitting on my lap throughout the journey looking out of the bus window and wondering what to expect at the Institute. We approach a steep narrow road and pass by the front of the Institute – a large grey old building, which puts a sense of fear in me. We drive to the side of the building which appears to be the drop-off and pick-up points. The families on the bus adopt a routine and help their children from the bus. The bus driver, a stern looking man attempts to help some families, as the language barrier prevents the parents explaining it is better for them to help their own children.

Carrying Dana and her walking sticks we enter the building and walk to the third floor, up a large grey concrete staircase. We hear the chatter of student conductors talking in Hungarian and see other parents chatting in their own native language and with familiarity, heading towards where they need to be. We, as new parents, make our way to the office of the head of department. There, a large lady with a confidence and authority greets us and introduces herself as the head of department. To be honest, my first impression is that I am feeling quite scared and want to take Dana back home. She speaks in a good English accent, asking us questions about Dana and her CP, I find myself answering as if I was in school. She tests Dana's range of movement and confirms the benefits she feels Dana will gain from attending the Institute. She explains about the class sizes and the ratio of contactors to children. The concern I have is that I am not allowed to be with Dana during any therapy. This is a rule that is adhered to and it is felt the children work much better without parents. I am apprehensive. After all, Dana is the youngest at only two and a half years of age. I have to put my trust in the conductors and think of the improvements I will see in Dana after the four-week programme.

We are shown to Dana's class and allowed to stay for a while, just until we settle Dana in. The class size is small and the ability of the children is similar to Dana, all walking with frames or sticks. We sit Dana on a bench as all the children are sitting in a semi circle and told we will see her later. She starts crying and I cannot bear to leave her. One of the conductors comes and also comforts Dana and assures me she will be OK; it is fine for us to leave. I find this really difficult as my instinct as a mother is to pick her up, give her a cuddle and make everything OK. Yet, I was being told to leave and told Dana will be OK. I had to think it was Dana's first day at school and if she cried there I would walk away. This was different though, as we are in another country and Dana is only two and a half years of age.

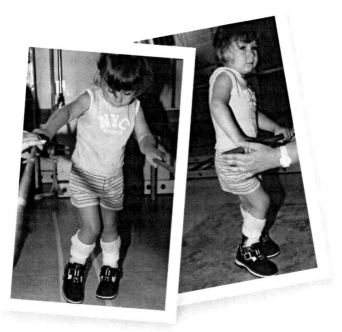

Learning to walk and balance at the Peto Institute

I leave the room hearing Dana crying and screaming, and it takes all my strength to keep walking. I have feelings of guilt and question myself on what I am doing. As I walk down the stairs I still hear Dana crying and I stop midway and think that I can't leave her; I must go back. If I do go back and take her home, how will I ever know what the benefits of this therapy will have on Dana? Walking away was the hardest thing and I then focus on picking her up soon. I will see how today has gone and make my decision to stay or go home. I have to detach myself emotionally, which may sound insensitive, and focus on this being the best therapy for Dana, or so I believe at the time.

I am back at the Institute in plenty of time as the day's session is due to finish at 3pm. I nervously wait outside the door and all I think of is cuddling her, hoping she has settled down and enjoyed some of the day at least. As I walk in with the other parents, I see Dana sitting and she seems happy. Giving her a big cuddle, I ask lots of questions to the conductors who say that Dana had worked hard and joined in well. To say I was relieved is an understatement, I didn't want Dana to go through this if it was making her scared or upset. As a parent this was a difficult decision, knowing if it is right for Dana, for the long term. Effectively our lives at home had to be put on hold for the time we were in Budapest. Dana was taken out of nursery and as parents we had taken time off work. We had to adjust to family life in a strange country for a month; shopping, cooking, washing and learning Hungarian, I always carry my Hungarian translation pocket book just in case. At least at weekends we spend time as a family doing fun things. So for the next four weeks, Monday to Friday, we make the daily trip to and from the Peto Institute. During the day Dana has a mid-morning snack, which consists of ham or cheese in a roll which will sometimes fill her up for her lunch. The children are well looked after; they have lots of food during the day, which they burn off as they work really hard during the days.

We fill our evenings gathered around the communal area in the hotel, chatting. Families cook and it is common to visit each other's apartment. One mother in particular who has been coming to Budapest for a number of years, makes delicious cornbread and shares this among families.

At the end of each block visit, the lead conductor of the group presents a report on progress achieved and recommendations. This type of therapy is to be included in daily life. I must continue this therapy myself at home using the same type of equipment because the progress made in just four weeks is incredible. Dana is a lot looser and I find her stretching easier to do. The conductors recommend a cream that is applied before therapy to massage into the muscles in order to warm them up and I find myself buying enough cream to last a while.

Enjoying the sunshine in Budapest

We find ourselves bringing Dana back to Budapest over the following six years and incorporating a summer programme. The summer programme is tailored slightly differently as there is a maximum number in one class and activities outside the Institute are arranged for the children, such as swimming and horse-riding. I do make it clear to the conductors I will be attending swimming and horse-riding also, which is accepted. The summer programme has a fun element and quite a few familiar conductors work with Dana. Dana builds a rapport over the years with her favourites and as parents we also have our preferences.

Over time the head of department is not so scary and in fact she is the most honest and caring person I have ever met. I can say she has had a major impact on Dana and has personally worked with her on many occasions. I am forever grateful to her for touching Dana's life and she will always be special to us as a family.

I discover through talking with parents in the hotel in Budapest that a centre in London is running with conductors from Hungary, setting up four weekly block sessions – the same format as in Budapest. Over the next six years we divide our time between Budapest and London, always going to Budapest in the summer for the summer programme. In the main, the London programme has UK families, with several travelling from around the world. For us though, it is a matter of travelling by tube or by car. Although it can be a very long day for Dana as the journey time each way is just under two hours, it is nice to get back to our own home each evening. By the time we join the London programme we are very familiar with the routine and of course expecting the same authoritative approach, I find a much more relaxed environment in London, where I am able to view Dana through a one-way mirror. I will often sit in the room after I have done the usual morning stretches on arrival with the mandatory cream, and watch Dana working through play. Dana is unaware I am able to watch her. Although she behaves well, she does tend to lose interest as her attention is focusing elsewhere, other than paying attention to the conductor. She is reminded to focus by the conductor and quickly pays attention. At the end of the day I admit to Dana I am able to see everything she is doing and we jokingly discuss the day's therapy on our way home. Her class group is again of a similar age and she soon becomes friendly with two girls, which is lovely to see. The travel and therapy soon become tiring for Dana and me, and we are glad when the block sessions come to an end.

Chapter 5

Meeting Dana's disabled needs

As most children get to the stage of beginning to walk and grow out of their strollers, I am at the stage of looking at a buggy that has to be sought from the same place as wheelchairs. The thought of this in itself is terrifying as this is the first introduction to specialist equipment for Dana. Although nervous at the thought of a 'special buggy', I have to think positively, as it is not a wheelchair and by the time Dana has outgrown the buggy she *will* be walking anyway. I have been given a telephone number to call by the physiotherapist in order to arrange an appointment to measure and test the buggy. Another service to become familiar with; I wonder, how many more services will there be in Dana's life?

The day of the appointment and I am feeling that this is a major turning point in Dana's life, and I do not know what to expect. Driving into the hospital I follow the signs to where I need to go until eventually I see the sign for the service which is waiting to see Dana. As I walk into the department, which was a children's ward in previous years, I imagine the ward filled with beds and staff nurses attending to children. The rooms are empty shells where a few office staff fill the space with office furniture. My attention is focused on what used to be the main ward and now is filled with buggies, wheelchairs and different types of equipment for children with a disability.

Dana starring in the nursery nativity play

As I walk in with Dana and a health professional, I confirm Dana's details. Yet another file with Dana's name on it and another set of notes sits on the desk. Selections of buggies are shown to

me for Dana to try. I sit Dana in each one and the health professional checks the fit and establishes Dana's sitting position is correct. The one chosen as suitable is similar to a stroller except the
width is slightly bigger and the feet positioning is higher allowing
the feet to be supported. All these differences are pointed out to
me; although important and it is vital for Dana to have the most
suitable buggy, I am still thinking this is not for long and Dana
will be walking soon.

Dana's disability is only noticeable when she is required to walk,
as she will walk with the aid of her sticks. Her character is happy
and smiling and she has the most angelic face. I often look at her
and just for a moment forget about her disability, and then the reality floods back and a wave of deep sadness comes over me. There
are things Dana will not experience: running in the snow in her
wheelies or simply walking to where she wants to go just because
she wants to. Strangers start to stare, because at Dana's age most
children are walking beside the stroller or holding mum's hand.
Dana though is in her 'special buggy'; this feels uncomfortable and
I hate the stares, especially those from adults. I rise above it and
focus on where we are going.

During Dana's younger years, the physiotherapist and portage
both recommend Dana has a standing frame to use at home. The
purpose of this is to keep Dana up in a standing position and able
to play. The standing frame is really heavy to carry and has a flat
plate for Dana to stand on and it can be positioned under a table so
Dana can play. This is used as part of physiotherapy for an hour a
day. The frame, made out of steel has a large strap that wraps around
Dana's waist and two leg straps that wrap just around each knee
area. Each time I place Dana in this stand it feels like a reaffirming
of her disability. I hate this feeling and keep thinking positively that
it is not for ever and this is only temporary. Dana didn't mind being
in the standing frame and I always have Bella to mimic standing up
straight, which helps.

The time we spend in Budapest and London also allows me to look at and assess the equipment that has benefited Dana. The therapy equipment used in the Peto centre did not always replicate the UK physiotherapy approach. I am keen to enhance what Dana had been used to in the Peto centre and had worked incredibly hard with during the block sessions. The physiotherapists in the UK are not of the same mindset and again I have to make a decision about what is best for Dana. As you can imagine, I am drawn towards what works and the results I had seen. With this in mind I buy a set of parallel bars, which Dana uses to practice walking and stepping up and down on a box. The physiotherapist's reaction is not complimentary and she cannot understand why I have wasted my money and bought these, even though I have clearly highlighted the superb work Dana achieves. It is definitely starting to feel that the physiotherapist has an idea of Dana's capabilities and I have mine. The two are not the same. I strive to get Dana what she needs to help her even if this means buying privately. I am Dana's mum and as far as I am concerned, there are no limitations.

Ballet

At home I am always looking for opportunities where Dana is able to experience new things and I find out that the gym I go to runs ballet classes. The classes run weekly so I speak to the teacher and ask if Dana will be able to join. I think the influence of watching the Tweenies has a positive impact and Dana is so excited when I tell her she'll be joining the class from this Saturday.

I am informed of what outfit to buy and take Dana shopping. At this point she is so excited and by the time we get home, she can't wait to try everything on. Looking at Dana all dressed in the ballet outfit, for a split second I forget about the disability and my mind takes me back to the hopes and dreams I had for Dana during my pregnancy. Coming back to the moment I smile as Dana stands so proudly with her sticks, she looks like a ballerina – beautiful.

Dana dressed and ready for her ballet class

Saturday, the day of Dana's first lesson brings a mixed feeling of excitement and nervousness on my part. Dana is just so excited – dressed in the full ballet outfit with her hair in a ponytail. As I carry Dana and the sticks up two sets of stairs to the gym studio, other girls, all dressed in similar outfits, arrive with their parents. The stares from the children and parents are all too familiar. That is not important, Dana attending her first ballet lesson is why we are here and we greet the teacher who explains the routine for each lesson. She is supportive in allowing me to help Dana with the lesson; however, during the lesson, Dana is happy walking alone with her sticks, although slower than the other children who are running around. Parents sit and chat while watching and a sense of envy comes over me. Dana is happy, smiling and having fun and that's all that matters. She particularly enjoys watching herself in the floor-to-ceiling mirror. At the end of each lesson the teacher compliments the effort made by all the children and invites each girl to receive a sticker for good work. Dana walks with her sticks when the teacher calls her name and receives a sticker, which she is very proud of. I also am incredibly proud of her achievements and as I ask her if she enjoyed herself, she replies by asking if she can go again the following week. Of course she can.

Chapter 6

Starting preschool

A T age three I feel Dana needs to be around other children, and although she had been to toddler groups, it is time for a more formal setting. I want a preschool that does not have too many children, which may sound strange but I am concerned about other children running around and knocking Dana over. I am also looking for a setting that has a comfortable feel and where the relationship between staff and children is good. I visit many nurseries over several months. Some I walk in and walk straight back out again, others I take my time questioning staff and observing the children. I look around and see if any children are sitting alone, and instantly think I do not want this to be Dana. The key element is how the preschool will deal with Dana's disability and fortunately they all have a very positive approach. This is a relief, as you can imagine, as I was preparing myself for the worst.

The particular nursery we choose for Dana to attend, on the initial visit, I know instantly is the right setting for Dana. The staff are so friendly and the relationship with the children is caring. The structure during the day includes playing inside and in the garden, reading, drawing, painting, pretend play and writing. There is always an event taking place; Easter egg hunts, celebrating special occasions, making decorations and costumes. One Christmas for the nativity play, Dana is chosen to play Mary. As I sit in the audience there is a mixture of crying and laughter as Dana held a doll, who was baby Jesus, upside down and then dropped him. Fortunately the other children sitting by Dana are able to pick up the doll without disturbing the play too much. I cry seeing my little girl being part of a play like her friends; it is lovely to see the conversations of whispers between Dana and the other children.

Dana in her bedroom after a busy day at nursery

Over the months and years Dana attends nursery, staff are so approachable and accommodating, and Dana is comfortable enough to say how she feels. Dana wears a uniform consisting of a skirt, polo shirt and a jumper. It feels very strange seeing Dana wear a uniform at such a young age even though she looks adorable. Her shoes, which are bought for nursery and have to fit her splints make her disability noticeable. How I hate seeing the splints on Dana. I can't use my usual tactic and put her in trousers. It feels her disability is on show and for the first time she is in a school setting. Each morning I drive to the nursery, I park up and walk Dana in with tripod sticks. The sticks are quite heavy and I often wonder how wonderful it is that she mastered the use of them. A member of staff is assigned to look after Dana specifically and as a result Dana is able to go into the garden and ride a bicycle or just play. What is really great, is that Dana is like the other children; she just needs a bit more help. The nursery always views Dana like any other child; things may take a bit longer for her to do or she may need a bit more assistance than the other children, but there are no barriers placed. I am very fortunate to meet some of the loveliest people who are part of Dana's early years.

Big School

After a couple of years at the nursery it is time for Dana to move to 'big school'. Saying goodbye is the hardest thing to do, as the staff have become friends and have been such an integral part of Dana's life.

I always knew when the time came for Dana to start school it was going to be in a mainstream school. However, I am being steered towards a special needs school as The Local Education Authority feel it may be easier on Dana being in a special needs school. I do not understand how this type of school will benefit Dana and to be honest I cannot see Dana in one. Dana is able to walk with tripod sticks, although I accept she requires assistance. Her communication skills are age appropriate and her disability is mobility. I want Dana to be around other children who do not have a disability and the mainstream schools now have to be inclusive of disabled children. At the same time I am advised that Dana must have a Statement of

Education Needs in order for the school to meet Dana's needs. The purpose of the Statement is that it follows Dana throughout her school life and advises on Dana's specific needs. The Local Education Authority requires reports from the professionals involved with Dana and from us as parents. Little did we know at this stage how much paperwork and form filling is going to be involved. As parents this is completely new to us and at times overwhelming. All I want to do is find a good school for my little girl to attend, just like any other mother. This process of form filling now is setting Dana apart from her peers and we have the documents to prove it. Is Dana now to be referred to in accordance to what is written about her? Seems heartless and compares to being on that hamster's wheel. Yet another 'system' Dana has joined, and I find myself getting even further into a different world, a world which talks a different language understood only by those who are part of it.

The schools we view are very different to the setting Dana had been used to in nursery. They, of course, are much bigger with a lot more children. I am starting to feel very nervous and to be honest I do not want her to go to any because I am scared. How will Dana manage? Will she make new friends? How will children react to seeing Dana differently? Will the children be kind to Dana and not be subject her to bullying? Still, with all this in mind, I know Dana will attend a mainstream school as she is bright and the disability affects her legs only. Acting as any other parent, we look to see which schools have the best academic results and focus our attention on these schools. I always imagined my child attending my primary school, yet, when I view the school through the eyes of a mum this time and not as a pupil, it is just not the right setting for Dana. I am disappointed Dana is not following in my footsteps; however, the main priority is finding the right school, which will meet all her needs.

The school we eventually choose has a very good reputation with good results and the head of the school is very proactive and supports our decision for Dana to attend her school. We meet on several occasions prior to officially starting school and Dana is assigned a support worker as stated in the Statement. The morning of Dana's first day at school I am feeling very apprehensive; having bought and labelled the uniform I help dress Dana in a grey skirt, white socks, white polo shirt and green jumper. She also has a green book bag. Having previously viewed the class Dana would be in, it seems much larger in size when I walk in with Dana. The class teacher greets us and welcomes Dana. Within moments we are joined by lots of other children also in the same class. Fortunately the assigned support worker is also in the classroom and comes to sit with Dana. I keep asking if she will be OK and is there anything the support worker or the teacher is unsure of. I know I have to trust them and let go of Dana but it is so hard. The initial time at school is mornings only, so this makes me feel reassured that within a few hours of dropping her off at school I will be back to pick Dana up. After a few weeks it is time for Dana to stay all day. Although at first it feels daunting, she does settle in really well at school and the support has been great. I am happy she has settled in well, however, parents will avoid talking to me as they see Dana walking with her frame or they will just stare. Worrying about who will stare is always at the forefront of my mind as I approach the school. I hide my true feelings from Dana as she is excited to go to school. Inside I am angry – on the outside – I am happily speaking to Dana about her day and the exciting things she has done. Dana is chatting away describing her day and I am listening at the same time knowing children and parents will be looking at her. School is always going to be different. I know this; I want Dana to mix with children of all abilities in a mainstream school, to be challenged and grow as an individual. This is the compromise I have to make; I have to put my child's educational needs first. There are no other children similar to Dana at school, no parent who is feeling what I feel. If only the parents understood for a minute what it feels like to be stared at or to be avoided – just for one minute – I wonder if they would think twice.

Dana at home continuing with physiotherapy holding onto parallel bars

Drama school

I was getting a sense Dana enjoyed singing and music and by the age of four I started looking at Stagecoach. We visited the school and as we walked around, each room had different aged students either singing, dancing or acting. There was an air of energy around and a sense of fun. I knew I wanted Dana to be part of this. The principal welcomed us and invited Dana to attend a trial morning to see if she enjoyed it. I was pleased the school accepted Dana and discussed with her the practicalities of each class and how we felt she would cope. I felt a sense of normality; I was like the other parents who bring their children to Stagecoach. Dana would be learning new skills and having fun. I was still worried how she would feel being with strangers and how the other children would treat her. What if the children were horrible, as Dana could not dance as they could? What if Dana was crying all the time she was there? I wouldn't know. Still, attending Stagecoach was a good thing and I put those thoughts to the back of my mind.

On the day of the taster session I arrive with Dana and we are introduced by the teacher to a class of children similar age to Dana. All the children are sitting dressed in the obligatory uniform and Dana is asked to sit beside a little girl. Sheepishly I walk out and leave Dana, yet inside, the worrying thoughts return. The principal reassures me that Dana will have fun and will be fine. The fact was, I had to let go and could not keep her with me all the time. Dana had to be exposed to other experiences, it was important for me to get her to try out new things, despite her disability. It was vital for me to keep things normal, I still was not accepting Dana's disability and wanted her to do what other children her age were doing. After a few hours I practically ran back to the school and peered through the window of the classroom being careful Dana didn't see me. A sense of relief came over me as I caught sight of her sitting among the other children laughing. The principal caught me looking in and said how much Dana had enjoyed the class. She was enrolled straight away and started a few weeks later. We discuss Dana's disability further and are reassured Dana will have someone to look after her. This is such a milestone and it feels that Dana will really benefit from attending Stagecoach. Not only will Dana be learning something new, she will also build on her confidence and self-esteem. As I look at the order form to buy the uniform required, I am instructed by Dana that I have to buy the plimsolls as she has to have the full uniform. I order the full uniform including the plimsolls, which means she is unable to wear her splints. Although I dislike the splints, I accept that they do serve a purpose which is to keep her feet flat and in the correct position.

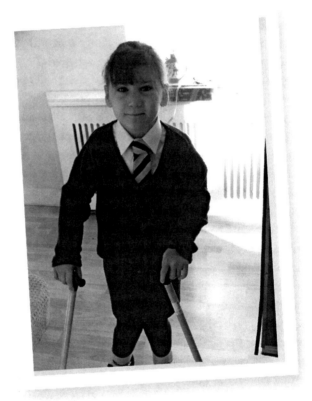

Dana ready for school

The first day of attending Stagecoach is filled with a mixture of excitement and apprehension. Dana is feeling excited and I am apprehensive. As I dress Dana in the full uniform, black leggings, black sweatshirt and the mandatory plimsolls, I feel a sense of pride and if I am completely honest a sense of normality. Parking in the school car park, I see other parents with their children of different ages arrive and go into their classes. Now I am feeling very nervous and talk to myself, saying how much fun Dana will have. As I walk into the school carrying Dana and the sticks, the principal and teachers greet us and welcome Dana introducing us to her helper, a bubbly and cheerful teenager who will be with Dana during the lessons. During the weeks and months that follow, Dana is learning words to sing and even acting. Taking part in dance classes is difficult and she does her best with her helper on hand to assist. Dana is included in everything.

Over time it becomes clear that the plimsolls are not suitable and Dana will need to wear her splints and we ensure we buy black trainers to fit in with the uniform. I attend small productions every so often and remember on one of these occasions that all the children and Dana are dressed up in animal costumes. Dana is dressed as a lion and plays the part very well. I am so proud of my little girl and have my camera clicking at every opportunity. The proudness is always coupled by a sense of sadness seeing Dana needing help and not being free to move as the other children are able to.

Dana is awarded achievement medals that represent the length of time spent at Stagecoach. These are presented at the end of term productions. Again, as the only child who has a mobility disability, these awards show great strength and determination on Dana's part In the six years Dana spends at Stagecoach Dana is liked by the teachers and popular with children of all ages, which is a relief. Her confidence grows and her skills in acting and singing are beginning to show. I want to encourage Dana to develop the things she enjoys and enrol her in extra singing lessons. The school is always full of praise and encouragement and very much follows the belief that anything is possible.

In drama, Dana passes a drama exam and receives an award, which is amazing and wonderful. It is incredible to think that Dana is developing in confidence, creating an identity, learning new skills and actually being very good. However, health professionals are not supportive and are surprised that we even thought of enrolling Dana in such a school, let alone attend one. My belief is not to accept someone is unable to do something until they attempt it, and Dana is no different. Anything is possible, if you have the correct mindset.

Junior School

From the early stages of Dana's school life, it is clear that she has to conform as the years progress. There are, however, areas where she is a bit slower to conform – or is it just easier to get the support worker to aid her? Discussions take place in meetings at the school to look at ways to tackle areas of concern. The solutions always appear to be the easiest, and not as I feel, the most appropriate. As Dana develops through the school her writing is not as quick as other children and therefore she is not able to produce as much work. Rather than look at ways to improve her writing ability, the school suggest using a laptop that will solve the problem. At this time, Dana's typing skills are as you can imagine not very good and she will search for the letter and press the key one finger at a time. Of course using a computer takes Dana more time to type, and more importantly, my feeling is she needs to improve her writing skills using pen and paper, not a computer. I feel very strongly that Dana is more than capable of holding a pen and is able to write, therefore she just needs to practice more than other children to improve. It is very easy to think this is an area where Dana is pigeonholed, placed in a category of slow writers, and therefore using a computer is easier. This is not right and I firmly state that I do not want Dana using a computer. After all she is only eight years old and I want her to learn the basic skills. Meetings are held regularly with professionals involved with Dana, from health to social care and each person attends and discusses their findings or observation of Dana. As a parent I listen and question their opinions.

The first time I attend one of these meeting, it feels very strange discussing Dana and listening to other people's opinions and recommendations. It is fair to say Dana has a label of Special Needs and with this label comes different professionals, who input into Dana's school life. As a mum, Dana is an individual who has a disability and her ability to do what she is capable of doing must be encouraged. The comprehension and understanding the disabled needs within the day-to-day school life is not appreciated, and as a result, Dana is restrained from developing naturally. Everything in school is made easier for her, so how can she learn, when something is difficult, to problem solve. Quite simply she doesn't. Someone will do it for her. So over the years Dana has relied on others, teachers and peers to problem solve on her behalf. It saddens me that this is the culture and it is not blame on any individual, it is a fact through understanding a child's individual disability, you are developing the child as a whole person.

The trend is on finding the quickest solution. As a parent I find myself disagreeing with the suggestions made. Most of the support workers looking after Dana on a one-to-one basis are caring towards her, which makes a very big difference. Knowing your child is being cared for well in such a busy environment is reassuring. One particular support worker stands out personally. She understood Dana and allowed her to do things for herself that Dana may have previously found difficult. Over the time Dana spent with her, Dana's confidence grew. The support worker's bubbly nature and her positive approach to Dana made school life for me that little bit easier. I knew it was more than just a job for this lady; Dana had bonded so well and she liked her as she took an interest in her needs. This support worker was with Dana for a year, as the school decided it was in Dana's best interests not to get too familiar with the same person so she was allocated someone completely new. Not new to the school of course, but for Dana she was new. This is one of those examples, which made no sense to me. Dana was developing in confidence, had a support worker who fully understood her needs and, most importantly, Dana had a bond with her. The new term in school is spent with the new support worker getting to understand Dana, and as a parent, I feel I am starting from scratch again.

A family evening out

As I drive Dana to school and park in my usual place in the staff car park, I see the other mums walking to school with their children. It is walk to school week and the children are taking part. Dana is unable to take part, although she does have her walker and walks to her class with her support worker who meets us at the school gates. At the end of the school day, I park in the same spot, and this time mums stand outside the school gates patiently waiting for their children to finish for the day. They chat to each other and inside I feel jealous. I want to be standing with them talking, not waiting in the allocated spot of the staff car park. I have a deep sinking feeling; if only things had been different, if only Dana wasn't disabled. Although it may not appear important, for me being part of standing at the school gates is important and over the months and years the divide becomes deep rooted. Dana is different and people for whatever reason are uncomfortable speaking to me. The sense of loneliness becomes common and the stresses of juggling school with appointments are ever increasing. Watching Dana's face as she walks with her support worker to where I am waiting for her, it is clear she is delighted to see me and excitingly tells me what she had done in school. I'm glad Dana is accepting of where I meet her and is not asking why I am not with the other mums.

Dana is progressing well at school academically. The fact that she is able to fit in so much in her young life and still achieve very good reports from junior school is a credit to her. During her junior years she develops friendships from the infants' school and her friends have grown up with her disability. Her friends do not see her any different apart from mothering her a bit too much, which is out of kindness.

Chapter 7

֍ ֎

Developing Dana's confidence

From the moment Dana was diagnosed I vowed that I would never give up hope, and I will do whatever it takes to make thing better for her. As a person I become stronger. I realised from very early on it is my responsibility to look after Dana's needs and take control. Professionals give their opinions based on their knowledge, it doesn't mean I have to accept or agree with what they are saying.

With the internet having become my best friend, I will always research something I do not fully understand or agree with. I feel a sense of empowerment and as a mum become an expert on my child. Often the health professionals say no to other therapies suggested to help Dana. Yet surely there must be something somewhere we both agree with. One thing I am sure of is that Dana is not going to end up using a wheelchair for the rest of her life as we have previously been told. I am not sure how, but I know I will find a way. Doing nothing is not an option.

Ironically the disability complemented Dana's acting ability as she is put forward for auditions and is winning the roles. Dana is signed with an agency and the jobs come in one after another. She does various photo shoots promoting awareness for a variety of organisations and major national annual campaigns. Commercials are filmed either in the studio or an outside location depending on the topic type. TV roles including working for Children's TV, she enjoys and particularly working on live TV.

Dana in costume appearing on live children's television

Leaving home to arrive at the studio means we have to leave at 5am, as the TV show is airing live later in the morning. I have become an expert at packing a bag when Dana has a booking; with hairbrush, change of clothes, tissues, itinerary for the job and directions of venue. We arrive at the studios and are shown to a waiting area, which has a wall covered with flat screen TVs showing the live show. We are told we can stay here while Dana is filming or stand at the side of the set. Dana is so excited and I am pleading with her to listen to what is being asked of her, as it is live TV. She is not able to start again, and what she says is aired live to thousands of people.

It is time for Dana to get ready on set and she is introduced to the children's TV presenters. I am standing at the side of the set watching a smaller TV monitor nervously looking at her every move. Dana interacts with the presenters and has to read out a story. The presenters ask Dana questions about the story and Dana answers perfectly. Nothing is scripted although Dana knows what she has to do. The next few hours pass by so quickly and Dana does a fantastic job and is beaming when she finishes filming.

Dana is put forward for other TV roles, some are more successful than others and if there is an audition I always encourage Dana to do her best. It's all experience for her and more importantly I want her to enjoy what she is doing.

A car picks Dana and me up from home and drives us to the studios for filming. Dana is particularly excited as we reach the studios and we are shown to her dressing room. A member of staff comes and chooses one of the many dresses I have in my bag for Dana to wear on set, to iron. We are both very well looked after and Dana is enjoying every minute. Dana is dressed and ready for filming to begin. As I sit on the seat, where the audience would sit, with the producer of the show, I am amazed how confident Dana is at acting and filming the scenes with a famous actress. Dana is not fazed one bit. During a tea break in between filming, one of the crew comes round offering doughnuts for everyone. Just before this Dana is discussing the wig the actress is wearing and sends her assistant to collect another wig from her dressing room. Meanwhile, Dana has picked up a doughnut to eat. I am watching her while I still chat with the producer and the assistant arrives with the wig. I see Dana trying to work out what to do with the doughnut, as she wants to touch the wig. I then see Dana asking the actress to hold the doughnut, as she wants to hold the wig, fortunately wiping her hands beforehand. I sit very embarrassed and look at the producer who is smiling. The poor actress sits holding Dana's doughnut for a few seconds until someone takes it from her. In the car on our way home after filming, Dana and I are discussing the day and I ask her why she gave the doughnut to the actress to hold. Her reply: "Because I wanted to feel the wig."

I am incredibly proud of Dana and everything that she has achieved. I hope by believing in her, that anything is possible and by never giving up, she is now able to be confident in herself as an individual. Dana is an incredibly strong person who just so happens to have a disability. If I had listened to others who did not agree with exposing Dana to these outside experiences, she would not be the person she is today. As a mother I learnt very early on to take control and responsibility. I do not want others deciding what is best for my child and I certainly do not want my child cocooned in a closed environment.

Chapter 8

⇥⇤

Interventions and adaptations

EACH new splint fitting is coupled with a trip to the shoe shop, which is a challenge in itself. Imagine walking into a shoe shop and browsing the shoes, which seems fine, and perfectly natural. Now imagine when the assistant asks if I need help and looks at me strangely when she sees the splints. I explain the purpose of the splints and that the shoe must fit over them so she will need to measure the foot in the splint. I go through a large number of shoes and trainers, and on the floor around my feet are lots of shoe boxes. I am feeling hot and flustered. After exhausting all the girls' shoes and training shoes, and seeing the disappointment in Dana's face as the shoes she likes she can't have as they do not fit over her splints, we turn to the boys' section. For me again this reaffirms Dana's disability and deep down another piece of me falls deeper into depression. It may only seem just a shopping trip but this is not buying something you like, it has to fit around something that Dana has to wear because of her disability. I can't just buy my little girl pretty shoes, the ones she chooses. It's heartbreaking. I find a pair of black shoes for boys that fit the splint and look OK, and although Dana accepts this, I can see the disappointment in her face. I reassure her that this is not forever, and that it is only temporary.

At the back of my mind I am thinking in another few months or so I will have to start the whole process again.

The type of splints Dana wears vary and depend on how much support she needs. The cast made initially, produces long day splints and shorter ankle splints. Both cause friction and produce sores on her feet and a further appointment is needed for these to be corrected. This is usual, and the timescale in resolving this can take weeks. As you can imagine ensuring Dana has suitable splints which will not add any further problems is a priority, however, the fragmented process is both frustrating and unnecessary, which puts added pressure on us.

The balance in maintaining a normal routine is increasingly difficult as more pressure is placed on Dana to wear certain things and be at certain appointments. School and home life at times takes second place and with no additional support it falls to us as parents. The strain this can have is a gradual process as more demands are placed with Dana's disability. I fall deeper into depression and make the decision to see my doctor who refers me to see a counsellor. To the outside world I put on a front and hide how I really feel inside.

Dana's right leg and especially her right foot is increasingly getting worse and over a series of years, Botox has been used to temporarily address this. On the three occasions Botox has been performed, all have required Dana to be admitted as day surgery and the procedure done under general anaesthetic. The day of the procedure, Dana is booked in and has the pre-checks done in the children's waiting room. Quite a few children are waiting by this time in their hospital dressing gowns and with the hospital wristbands. The time for Dana to have the Botox procedure arrives and naturally she is scared, and I feel anxious. She starts to cry and does not want it done. Of course she doesn't; any child would feel this way. If I could choose not to have this done I would, as after all this is a toxin that we are agreeing to. However, the benefit outlined to me by the consultant is that with intensive physiotherapy, it will allow the weaker muscles to be targeted and overall improve her when we stretch.

We arrive at the pre-med room, Dana is already lying on the hospital bed and she fights the mask. A nurse and I calm her down and hold her as she is moving her head from side to side. I want her calm and not falling asleep agitated. The anaesthetist places the mask and Dana starts counting, and then she is asleep. The procedure is finished very quickly and Dana is soon in the recovery room and then transferred to the day surgery ward. Recovery is always problematic as the effects of the pre-med and the anaesthetic leaves Dana in a very grumpy mood when she wakes. Seeing her for the first time is always a relief, even if she is grumpy. For me she has come through the general anaesthetic and the procedure is over. Soon we can go home, once Dana has eaten and fully recovered. Another visit to the hospital done and Dana leaves with a full-legged plaster that she must wear for six weeks.

I find when Dana has a plaster that this masks her disability, as it is seen as being normal. If there are no splints to wear, then for me, Dana does not look different. Being in plaster for six weeks means that physiotherapy is also limited; however, after six weeks have passed, then intensive physiotherapy is required given that Botox has a very short time limit. To ensure that intensive therapy is in place before Botox is given can create a problem, as Dana's needs do not always match the therapist's availability. Having seen my daughter undergo a procedure under general anaesthetic and the pain that she endured, the fact that she has to wear a plaster for six weeks without the post intensive physiotherapy, adds further strain to already stressful circumstances. I feel as if I have to justify Dana's needs and why they are so important.

While Dana is in plaster and as she is older, she requires a more supportive walking aid and a posture walker is recommended. Again this is requested and takes months to arrive. The posture walker is a frame that assists Dana's posture when she walks. As she grows, she will require a slightly bigger model. The frame is used for school and walking at home.

The effects of Botox have certainly disappeared and after a few months, my concern increases over Dana's right knee turning inwards, which has an impact on her right foot also turning inwards. I reach the stage where I am unable to place Dana's right foot into her splint. I see the deformities developing before my eyes, so they are not an overnight surprise. At each hospital appointment I raise my concerns and I keep getting the same reply: "This is how Dana's cerebral palsy is affecting her." Does nobody care except me? Am I so naïve about Dana's condition, I should expect this to happen? I seem the only person alarmed at what I am seeing. Looking at Dana's foot, this does not look comfortable or pleasant – surely this can't be right. There is no solution to address the knee turning inwards, and the only solution given to me to address the foot is for Dana to have a tendon release surgery to straighten it. How did we get to this stage, as on previous hospital appointments I keep raising this concern? I feel angry and let down that suggestions were not given before and this has resulted in the need for a painful surgical procedure. Dana's leg will be in plaster for six weeks again following surgery and then the normal infrequent number of physiotherapy sessions will continue.

Making the decision for a wheelchair

Unfortunately as Dana is growing, the spasticity in her body is taking its toll. Her legs are becoming tired more quickly. Her posture is starting to deteriorate, and her knees are going inwards more. Dana starts to find difficulty in walking longer distances and also standing for more than five to ten minutes. The day arrives which I have been dreading; the thought of Dana needing a wheelchair is a reality. I have fought for so many years not to let this happen and have ignored those around me when they have suggested Dana would be better in a wheelchair. I didn't think so, and what would that mean for Dana? Once in a wheelchair that's it for life? I envisaged the early years, thinking that one day Dana would be walking down the aisle on her wedding day, with daddy so proud arm in arm. The hurt to this day has emotionally crushed me of all the hopes and dreams for my little girl. Thoughts of her dancing at her school prom are now not an option. I was not supposed to let this day happen. Now I have to face the facts that for Dana's well-being and as others have commented for her 'independence', a wheelchair is the best option for her.

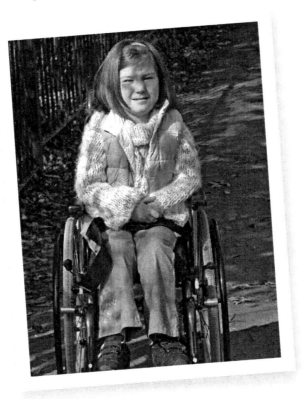

Dana in her wheelchair

An appointment is arranged with the same person who fitted Dana with the special buggy. Walking back into the same room, this time my focus is on the wheelchairs, I feel sick. As the health professional walks in with a child's wheelchair I start to cry. Crying for everything we have done in the past with Peto, all the procedures and of course all the physiotherapy. I am crying also for Dana's future, and the unknown. Do we need to move house into a bungalow, so it is all one level for Dana? What other adaptations do I need to do? How will Dana be independent as she grows into a teenager and a young lady? All these are questions I ask myself in a matter of minutes as Dana sits in the wheelchair, blank and clinical looking – looking lost. I want to make it all better, but I can't. I hate seeing her sitting there. I smile on the outside as I want Dana to see me happy and it is her special chair that she can wheel herself 'independently.'

Inside a bit of me died today. I have to come to terms with Dana's disability, as the wheelchair is now the end – but I don't want to. Her body is deteriorating and her muscles are unable to support her walking for long periods of time. This is the hardest decision I have made and feel I have let Dana down, as I had always made a promise of never allowing her to have a wheelchair. The fact is I have to think of Dana's needs and not my personal views. Of course Dana's needs always come first and I only wish there was another alternative, unfortunately there is not and Dana transitions from sticks to walking frame, to ultimately being in a wheelchair. I make a promise that if Dana has to have a wheelchair, then she is going to have a say in what it looks like. Within a few weeks we are in Kent looking at different models of wheelchair that are coloured to your own specification. Dana is excited to choose her own wheelchair and I am pleased at least it is something she has a decision over. The order is placed and Dana will receive her new chair within the next six weeks.

My sessions with the counsellor have ended and although useful, to be honest I make the decision during the counselling sessions to look at alternative methods. I start by looking at my fitness and decide to start running. Although difficult at first as I make excuses not to go running, the more I focus and am really strict with myself, the easier it becomes habit. I want to get better and working on my well-being is the first step. Don't get me wrong, this is not a miracle cure; however, it certainly helps me when I start to feel low.

Chapter 9

Friends

As Dana is my first-born I feel it important for her to mix with her peers. Even from an early age at the postnatal groups before and after diagnoses, Dana was a sociable child who would mix well with others her age. The disability is a factor which means she is unable to run around, yet she can play house and pretend to play shops or sit on the floor and play with dolls for example. She is just not able to walk around independently. Establishing friendships is important and more so for Dana to mix with all children. I want Dana to be exposed to all environments and not exclude her.

I accept all the invitations in her younger years when invited to birthday parties. The parties that are held in the children's homes are easier to cope with than the ones held in activity play centres. I dread reading where the party venue is, as I always have to plan to arrive early and always stay with Dana during all the activities. The activity play centres are particularly difficult and challenging for Dana and myself, as on arrival all the children run off and start climbing the large Jungle Gyms. It almost feels like a stampede, while I just stand back out of the way and watch, feeling upset Dana is not able to do the same. Dana does not miss out and I carefully place her on the apparatus. I join in and start climbing with her, crawling through tunnels and sliding down slides. I am the only parent on the activity frame and as I look down, how I envy the other mothers sitting and chatting while their children play. They do not have to worry about their children; I feel jealous and angry. Being with Dana as she is enjoying herself is more important and I hide my feelings well. On the outside I joke with the other mums how hot I feel climbing the frame and how this is keeping me fit. On the inside, I despair at how none of the mums are aware of how I must be feeling.

Dana at her Tweenie themed birthday party and at her make-up birthday party

At school Dana is popular even from infant age and it helps, as she continues her friendships with the same girls through junior age.

As far as her friends are concerned, Dana is who she is and they do not see or treat her differently. This shows me, as a mother Dana will have true friends, which I hope, will grow into lifelong friendships.

On each of Dana's birthdays I organise a party, making each one special and different. I always seem to be very fortunate with the weather and manage each year to have the parties outside at our home. For Dana's third birthday I organise a Tweenie themed party with a bouncy castle in the garden. I hire small tables and chairs for children to sit and eat and all the tableware and accessories are Tweenie themed. Adult family members and other parents help themselves to a barbecue, which is skilfully managed by Glen. Children sit and eat from individually made Tweenie party boxes and within minutes are finished, and they are running around and jumping on the bouncy castle. Dana stays with family members who play and sing with her, until I bring out the Tweenie birthday cake and we all sing Happy Birthday. Dana's face is full of smiles and pleased when she blows out the candles...with a little help.

As Dana grows the parties become more appropriate and for her seventh birthday, Dana suggests having a make-up party. A list of friends is created and the birthday invites are sent out. The theme is based on a fairy tale and I decorate the conservatory in pink organza and fairy lights. A company who specialises in children's make-up parties is booked for a few hours. The company arrives and set up in the garden; again the weather is sunny and warm and ideal for the party. A short time later the children arrive, all girls, who are so excited and quickly say goodbye to their parents. It's not long before all the girls gather around to look at the make-up and start discussing what colours they are going to choose. Dana is first in line and has a pretty pink and blue butterfly on her cheek with some blue eye shadow to complement it. The adults are eating, courtesy of Glen's usual barbecue skills. Dana walks around using her sticks and her friends are comfortable around her. Seeing Dana mix with her friends is lovely and for me brings a sense of normality. As the party is based on a fairy tale, the party bags are made of organza, filled with heart sweets, lip-gloss, notepad, pencils, an eraser, and each girl receives one, together with a piece of cake as a thank you for coming to the party. The girls love them and go home with their parents chatting about how much fun they had.

I have always welcomed Dana's friends to play with her and wondered why she is not always invited to play at her friends' houses. During the junior school years, Dana would ask if she could play at certain girls' houses after school. I always agreed, yet the invitations were not forthcoming. When I was Dana's age I remember dressing up and experimenting with make-up. Running around and going up and down the stairs, having the freedom to just go from one thing to another at a moment's notice because we decided to do so. I know it was not going to be the same for Dana and maybe the parents are a bit unsure, as they know she is unable to do this. Two of the school mums invited Dana over to their houses to play. The first is for tea after school and I stay with Dana helping her up the stairs, as she wants to play with her friend. It is an exciting feeling as I sit and talk to another mum as Dana is playing with her friend. I feel normal taking Dana to a friend's house and just sitting and talking, something that I never do. We talk about Dana's disability, which is quite liberating explaining life for Dana and how difficult she finds things to a mother who hasn't experienced this. She comments on how Dana is a happy and well-mannered little girl, which I am pleased to hear. After tea it is time to go home; Dana has had a lovely time and very much enjoyed going to her friend's house to play and have tea. That was the first and only time Dana was invited.

The second invitation is at another friend's house for a sleepover, which I must admit I am very anxious about. Dana is very excited as you can imagine, and pleads with me for days to go. I speak with the mother and explain what assistance Dana will need and she explains that the girls (four in total), will be in her daughter's room and Dana will sleep in the bottom bunk bed. Having sleepovers is what girls do, and Dana is no different, except that she will need a bit more help than the other girls. Dana has to go to stage school the next day and I inform her I will be arriving early in the morning to pick her up. I ensure Dana is fine and the mother feels comfortable and I say goodbye with mixed emotions. Worried about how Dana will manage and also how the other girls will act towards her, I hope she is not left out. Arriving back at the house in the morning, it is very quiet as I approach the front door. The mother answers the door and tells me that the girls are still asleep. They had been eating and chatting until the early hours and of course they are still sleeping. I walk into the girls' bedroom and all four girls are fast asleep. As I slowly wake Dana, she is not in a happy mood when I say she has to get up and go to stage school, although it is a Saturday. I am pleased she had a good time and again experienced a sleepover, more importantly the girls really didn't make Dana feel different. That was the only time Dana slept over at a friend's house.

For Dana's ninth birthday (and as she seems to have a few close friends by now), I arrange for a small number of friends and Dana to be driven in a limousine to Hamleys and then for a birthday celebration at the Hard Rock café. By this stage Dana is in a wheelchair and the limousine company are fantastic in accommodating the wheelchair and our needs. The girls are so excited as they arrive with their mums at our house. Outside, the limousine has arrived and the girls pose for pictures as parents take out their cameras.

Sitting in the limousine, the girls are giggling and taking pictures of each other. Looking at Dana as she joins in laughing, I think to myself, these are the memories I want her to have. Being with her friends and talking about girly things. How fortunate Dana is to have such a nice small group of friends. I can't help myself overhear how the girls are comparing their feelings of school and recalling events, which had recently happened. It reminds me fondly of myself at Dana's age laughing and joking with my friends and a memory that will last forever. The journey to London takes just under an hour and on the way I had already asked the driver to pass by Big Ben and the Houses of Parliament before reaching Hamleys, which he does much to the girls' delight. They look at the sights in wonder as they point out the landmarks to each other. Within a short time we have stopped outside Hamleys and to say all the girls are excited is an understatement. As we are getting out of the limousine I wonder how the girls will deal with Dana being in a wheelchair, as this is the first time she has been out with any of her friends.

Once Dana is settled in the wheelchair and before we venture inside the store, I set a few ground rules, mainly not to run off in the store and keep together. Although Glen is with me, we have been only used to caring for Dana, and now we have responsibility of four other able-bodied girls, so I am a little nervous and possibly overprotective. I must just relax and enjoy this experience; after all, it is Dana's birthday and of course I want it to be special. As we enter the store heading for the girls' department we pass through the wonders of Hamleys, listening and looking at the girls as they absorb everything. Pushing Dana in her wheelchair, the lift doors open, we are on the floor of the girls' department, and the girls rush out and head in different directions. I direct Glen towards one set of girls who have seen something they like and I keep up with another group and Dana. So much for the little pep talk earlier I thought to myself – this is going to be a challenge. The girls include Dana in everything they are looking at, trying hats on each other. I take a back seat as they take turns to push Dana around, which she appears to enjoy. After a few hours, although it does feel much longer, I am exhausted and it is time for lunch at the Hard Rock café.

With Hamleys shopping bags in the girls' hands, the limousine is waiting for us outside the store. The driver greets the girls as they get in the limousine, their smiles as they look at the shopping bags, confirm that they had a good time. I am glad just to sit down.

Two tables have been reserved at the Hard Rock Café, one for the girls and one for Glen and I. Dana had given me strict instructions that we are not to sit with her and her friends, so I obey her wish. I walk the very short distance, holding Dana's hands through the restaurant to the table, which is a semi circle and Dana sits in the middle of the group. Food is ordered and the girls enjoy enormous portions and then want chocolate for dessert. How they ate it all I will never know. I am so pleased everyone is enjoying themselves and Dana is having a wonderful birthday.

Finally arriving home in the early evening, all the girls' parents are waiting. I remember the mums saying to me I was brave arranging the trip and now I know what they meant. Although I am extremely tired, it was important Dana had a birthday she wanted and was able to share her experience with her closest friends.

Since then Dana has not been invited to her friends' houses for playtime and comes home from school saying the girls who are her friends are going to each other's houses and she seems to be left out. I do not understand; have they fallen out at school? It appears they had not. So why is this exclusion happening. I thought as they had been together outside of school it will somehow make things easier. I am upset as a mother and can see how Dana is feeling. My instinct as a mother is to approach the girls and ask them why they do not include Dana, but of course I wouldn't do this. My upset soon turns to resentment and I start exploring ways to change the resentment to a positive approach. I speak with the school and ask how Dana integrates with her peers and the teacher confirms Dana is very sociable and has a close group of friends. I think perhaps if Dana invites her friends round to play, then this may help.

It actually ends up with three of her friends coming over for play and a sleepover. As this is a girly sleepover, I bought some pamper items for the girls to enjoy. I set everything up for them and end up joining in as Dana is getting into a bit of a mess. Again all the girls are giggling, enjoying themselves and getting along with each other. I have put how I was feeling at the back of my mind as clearly seeing Dana happy and having fun is giving the girls a chance to see that Dana is just like them at home and maybe this is what is needed.

Unfortunately history is repeating itself and since the sleepover again not one of her friends invites Dana back for playtime. In school time they all play nicely together, yet outside school there seems to be a fear in having Dana in their homes. Maybe it has to do with the limited amount Dana is able to do, surely if they are true friends this will not matter. Have the parents mentioned to their children about inviting Dana over to play or is it the parents that are nervous at having a child with a disability in their home? I would rather hear honestly from parents about any fears they have; yet what is more hurtful is the fact nothing is said at all. How can I help change pre-conceived ideas if others are not open? How do I explain this to Dana, who thinks her friends do not like her? As a mother this is heartbreaking to hear, I certainly do not want my child feeling this way and immediately feel I have let my daughter down. Had I over-compensated by having a limousine party for Dana and her friends? Should I not have allowed her friends over for a sleepover? All the things I did was to let Dana experience a normal sense of being a girl, enjoying time with her friends and more importantly, developing her social skills just like any other girl her age. Dana is no different; she just finds it more difficult to walk around than her friends. It feels to me Dana is being penalised for the way she is and not accepted for who she is. This hurts me more. I feel used at being so open with her friends and parents, making the girls feel welcome in my home.

I focus Dana's attention on how well academically she is doing at school and the agency still requests Dana for photo shoots and TV work. This is building her confidence as an individual and is positively also boosting her self-esteem. I reinforce to Dana that she is a very special individual with unique qualities and to draw on all the positive experience she has with her TV work.

By the start of secondary school, the 'friends' soon become very distant and still to this day I do not know the reason why they had excluded Dana. To be honest, this is not important and Dana knows and feels that part of her life is in the past. Dana starts school enjoying meeting new friends and soon develops friendships with girls and boys she did not know previously. She joins an outside youth club and attends every Friday evening. She mixes with disabled and non-disabled children of all ages and usually she just sits and chats. Other children choose playing football, or taking part in crafts or one of the many other activities on offer. The youth club is a great outlet for Dana to be around other children other than those at school and again this builds her confidence. This is another milestone in developing Dana's social skills with strangers without having us as parents around.

Chapter 10

✦✦

Growing up – the effects of disability

As Dana grows up this comes with challenges, although the amount of help she requires remains consistent. Her needs range from showering to getting dressed… anything that requires her to balance. Her body is becoming heavier and this puts a strain on my ability to lift her. Becoming independent is not going to be possible as her needs are so great; carrying things for her as she is unable to, get a glass of water, get in and out of the car herself, all examples of how her needs are consistent throughout her growth. In the home adapting her bedroom, bathroom and downstairs are all factors I assess in allowing Dana to move around our home. Adding handrails to enable her to hold on as she walks around her bedroom may seem a simple concept, yet for Dana it opens up a whole new world, even if it is just her bedroom. The rails are placed along the walls so she can walk holding on to get from one end to the other. At least she can explore and play with her toys in a different environment from downstairs.

The assistance that is given at home is also consistent with school and a one-to-one support worker is assigned to Dana. In the early years at school as Dana is using sticks or her walker, her safety within school is apriority although lessons are taught in one class-room and generally the safety concerns are at break times and any games lessons. As Dana moves into secondary school her mobility becomes worse, the scale of the school and the amount of class changes that are required, results in her using a wheelchair permanently during school time. The need to always have an adult to help Dana although necessary is also hindering her ability to develop as her peers are doing naturally. The phrase "children learn by their mistakes" is a good example of how this does not apply to Dana. Learning to walk through the eyes of a toddler whereby they stumble and may fall a few times is an example of children persevering until they have mastered the skill. Whilst they are mastering this skill, they are also exploring their environment and developing their social skills. Dana has been protected to a certain degree, although the situations which I have placed her in, has meant that she has adapted well. In school and especially in the classroom, Dana is able to be with her peers and communicate together. Outside in the playground is another matter, all of the children are able to run around and play, which causes upset as she knows from a very young age that she is different.

Using a wheelchair for a family outing

As parents we have instilled the belief that Dana has a disability – the disability does not have hold of Dana. We have encouraged and exposed Dana to age appropriate experiences that we hope will develop her attitude to life and believing that anything is possible. We have been honest and explained what type of disability she has. Hearing Dana ask me why she is unable to run around like her friends is one of the most difficult things to answer. Inside I am crying with pain and have flashbacks to the night of Dana's birth. On the outside I cuddle her and say she is very special and her legs do not work as well as the other children at the moment, but that one day they will.

The discussions become more in-depth as Dana grows and when she asks how she became disabled, again it is one of the most difficult things to hear. Guilt is my first reaction. Guilty for not being strong or vocal enough to have Dana delivered sooner. Guilt is an emotion I keep hidden and I keep to the facts and even say I was watching the Eurovision song contest when my waters broke. It seems easier for me to detach myself emotionally and speak of the facts of the night she was born. Inside I am tearing apart, all hidden from Dana's view. Anger at the events of that night and also of feeling I have to justify at every opportunity why I am suggesting equipment, therapy and even schools. It seems from personal experience that nobody takes into account how emotionally challenging having a child with a disability is for the family. Having gone through periods of depression throughout Dana's disability and at times feeling quite desperate, my comfort was helping myself to help Dana in never giving up. I have my strategies when I feel low and turn to running as a sense of release. The thought of *what if* is a common theme I think about as she is growing up, as she is at different stages of her schooling or the toys she plays with. As a mother and especially with a first born you have an ideal picture in your mind of how your child will be at certain ages and for me, months before Dana was born, I had a vision of her walking from her bedroom into mine on her own just because she wanted to. I know that day will come.

Dana's CP is starting to affect her body in ways that I didn't understand. Asking the health professionals why her foot is rolling in or her knees rub together, the reply is always the same: "This is how Dana's cerebral palsy is affecting her." Is that it? How is that comment supposed to help make it better for Dana? The truth is nobody knows the answer and more importantly I do not know how it feels for her having CP. Her body is changing and she accepts this because that is all she understands. As her mother I do not accept it and want to know how to make things better. The NHS would suggest Botox or keeping up with stretching and wearing the splints. The fact is we are doing all this and more, with Dana also attending the specialist therapy and her body is still deteriorating. Each review appointment I am repeating the same concerns, making suggestions that I think are reasonable, which are laughed at. Why is there no difference when I stretch Dana and her legs and feet feel so hard to move? I do not understand why she is deteriorating before my eyes and I am the only one who cares. That is until the day came when I physically cannot put Dana's foot into her splint as it has turned in so much I am unable to place it in the position of the splint. The only suggestion and solution is to have surgery – a tendon transfer. Why has it come to this? My upset turns to anger that it has now resulted in surgery, as it feels now there is no alternative. The surgery will enable the foot to be placed back into the splint.

Dana's growth spurts causes a negative impact on her muscles as all the stretching that is done to loosen Dana's muscles disappears. With each growth spurt I notice considerable amounts of tightness. It feels I am pushing against the tide and always going back to the beginning with stretches, never seeming to get to a stage where there are dramatic improvements. Depending on how much her feet have grown, will determine if new splints are required. I look at Dana's feet and see if her toes are nearing the edge of the splint as I have a good idea of how many weeks of growth Dana has left. As the process to get new splints is long and can take up to two months, I ensure I start the process early enough with this in mind.

Over the years as Dana grows a major concern which I start to notice is her posture and how her shoulders and back are starting to round. Again, pointing out my concerns to the health professional as this is not a sudden discovery and I mention this on several appointments. The response is always the same and the reason is placed on the walking aids she uses, the walker and sticks. I do start to wonder what else am I going to discover and I am getting the feeling as Dana is growing that I am finding I do not understand how her body is changing because of the disability. I was always told her disability is not one that gets worse. Clearly this is not what I am seeing, so either there is a miscommunication in my understanding to what the health professionals are stating or I am not asking the right questions. I decide to be very specific with those involved in Dana's care as I have to understand if her posture is starting to deteriorate now, and if so, how this is going to affect her in later life. What is it we have to do therapy wise to correct this now? If the walker and sticks are causing the problem, how do we stop this getting worse? I suppose I don't know what I don't know, and I need to find the answers to find a way to help Dana. If there is anything which will prevent her posture from getting worse and knowing what to expect in the future in relation to her growth development I need to know.

It all seemed too much again to take on board, her physical needs in addition to not knowing the unknown. How can I plan for the future? The health professionals take on board my concerns and recommended Dana has a Gait Analysis to assist in surgical decision-making. The recommendations in the report suggests Dana's level of mobility will most likely gradually deteriorate as she grows, resulting in increased dependency on using a wheelchair. The report also states her current level of limited mobility and early development of multilevel fixed deformity suggests that her future prognosis for even assisted walking is likely to be poor. The spasticity in Dana's body determines how her muscles will develop and although the stretching we do will help loosen them, the muscles will always have the spasticity, therefore will always be tight. For Dana in particular, her weakness is her right side and noticeably her right foot is smaller and her right leg is not as muscular as her left. The results left us somewhat shocked and speechless. Reading the words seem coldly written and as a matter of fact. There is no appreciation in acknowledging they are talking about a girl's future and as parents how we will feel reading this. As far as the report is concerned and ultimately the health professionals, Dana's future is confirmed as wheelchair bound for life.

Being a girl brings natural developments and in the first term of starting secondary school, Dana starts her menstrual cycle. I had been practicing and showing Dana how to look after herself during this time, as I will not always be with her. I feel she has to understand and take on the responsibility herself, as this is something she has to personally do. Dana understands what will happen and how it happens. I buy her a book about how a girl's body changes and she enjoys finding out details and asks lots of questions. My worry as always is school; how will Dana manage, and to be honest, I dread the day Dana will start her period. I have prepared her as much as I can, what I have not given any thought to is the mood Dana would develop. We clash often, now this can be to do with how she feels hormonally or it can be to do with her limited physical ability. I talk to work colleagues who have had girls a similar age to Dana who confirm it is just being a teenager; I'm not so sure it is wholly this, as I know Dana gets frustrated when she is unable to physically do things for herself. She will have what I call 'diva' tantrums mixed in with comments of "I can't do this". I see Dana as a teenager firstly and allow her to get on with things and only intervene when I can see she is not able to do it on her own. I do not see the disability and expect Dana to attempt to find a way to do things.

All her younger years Dana has been so reliant on adult assistance, whether at school, home, stage school and she has not learnt the ability to problem solve. This is an important aspect of growing up and we talk through problems she finds difficult. The disability is not an excuse and strategies are developed which work for Dana. Her personality is still a caring, thoughtful and happy individual who throughout her younger years has endured an enormous amount of medical input while still trying to maintain 'normal' school and home settings. Looking back at how tolerant Dana has been is a credit to her as an individual and has given her a strong will to succeed. She has overcome many challenges, many of which I will never comprehend how difficult it must have been, physically and emotionally. I am so proud to call Dana my daughter.

Chapter 11

⇥⇤

High school

THE transition from junior school to High school is something I am not looking forward to. I had printed a list of schools in our area, both private and state funded and marked the ones that initially had a good reputation and good results and of course I could see Dana attending. Academically it is important Dana is challenged and is in a school that endorses progression in a child's education. I expect Dana to go to university and this is something Dana also wants to do. She is interested in learning Law and being a lawyer and she is also interested in Psychology and being a child psychologist. Both careers I believe she will excel in. Dana has an incredible memory and can recall dates and events instantly. She will recall events which happened years ago and go into specific details, all of which I have no memory of, which does not impress Dana as she feels I must know what she is talking about.

I have to balance her academic needs while ensuring the school also meets Dana's disability needs, although all schools should have an inclusion policy, testament to this is actually when we attend the open days.

I attend the private schools individually, arranging meetings with the head teachers. Both of the private schools are inclusive and welcome Dana. During the meeting we discuss how the school is able to adapt its facilities to meet Dana's needs and I feel overwhelmed that the schools are prepared to do this as she is in her wheelchair. We are shown around each of the schools and I can immediately picture Dana at one of the schools more than the other, although both schools academically are excellent. I take all the information away to give further thought as I still have the open days to attend at the state schools I had selected to view. Over a period of two weeks I attend six open evenings for prospective parents. At each school, following my own personal process; firstly, I ask to speak with the head of SENCO, who is the person responsible for coordinating the needs of children with special needs. Speaking with the head of SENCO gives me an understanding of how the school includes children with additional needs and how their role has an impact on children. Secondly, we take a tour of the school just like the other parents, viewing classrooms and looking through a sample of current pupils' schoolwork. Walking around the school also gives me the opportunity to listen to the teachers and get a sense of how they interact with pupils.

One mainstream school I visit say that they are unable to accommodate Dana and this school cannot accept her. As you can imagine for a teacher to say this to me as a parent is shocking and I find it unbelievable that I am hearing this. Clearly this is not a school I want Dana to attend. Does this teacher not realise in addition to viewing schools, as other parents were doing for their own children to ensure it met a suitable academic level, I also have to ensure the school meets the needs of Dana's disability. As Dana will attend a mainstream school and as I mentioned previously, has a Statement of Educational Needs (SEN), which the Local Education Authority (LEA) must approve. Since I began the search for a suitable high school for Dana, the LEA have suggested Dana attend a particular school that is built to meet the needs of disabled and non-disabled children. I do not want Dana to attend this school as I feel it does not meet all her needs, not just her disability. Although I know that this school is not appropriate for Dana, I feel I have to justify my decision based on visiting this school rather than what I feel is right for her.

Choosing a school for Dana seems to be a battle, as I have to justify why particular schools are unsuitable. In addition, meetings are held with professionals involved with Dana towards the end of the junior school years to discuss the support needed at high school . The SEN is reviewed for accuracy and amended accordingly. The school that I clearly voiced as being unsuitable keeps appearing on the SEN and I repeatedly state this is not the high school for Dana. I feel strongly Dana should not be 'labelled' and expected to attend a particular school because it is easier to allegedly meet her disability, as the school is modern and all wheelchair accessible. It has got to a point in the process that I am prepared to home tutor Dana as the LEA keep insisting on this school. Every corner I turn I am faced with issues to deal with, which when accumulated are so stressful. Forms to complete, evidence to produce to justify my options, additional equipment that the junior school feel Dana needs and on top of this, ensuring the professionals involved with Dana actually do what is required of them. I feel angry that other parents of non-disabled children do not have to go through this. Their process is so much simpler; choose a school, get accepted at the school and start school. I am dreading the day Dana starts high school and it is so important the right school is chosen and support is in place. This is my priority.

We finished the process of viewing all schools, private and state and although one of the private schools was my first choice, Dana struggled when she spent a day at the school, although she enjoyed the day immensely.

The school we choose for Dana is a mainstream mixed state school, which has just under 2000 pupils. Above all the school has an inclusive approach, which meets Dana's additional needs and it has a good academic record. I feel I can justify my decision when speaking and recording this to the LEA. We are fortunate the head of SENCO for the school is very supportive and proactive in gaining an understanding of what is required to meet Dana's needs before starting school.

As Dana is in her wheelchair, consideration of how the classrooms are reached is assessed. I find out very quickly high school is very different as each lesson is held in different classrooms, whereas in junior school the children remain in one class.

Dana with brother Oliver

Dana is feeling very grown up and excited about starting high school . After buying all the required uniform, we go school shopping, buying a new school bag, which is suitable to hang over the handlebars of the wheelchair. School shoes are as usual the most difficult item to buy and we tour all the shoe shops in the neighbouring towns. We find a shoe shop, which in the window has suitable looking girls' school shoes. On entering the shop all the children's shoes are upstairs, so I browse the girls' section while leaving Dana seated downstairs. A shop assistant has noticed our predicament at Dana not being able to view the shoes herself. There is no lift in the shop, so the assistant helps me with selecting a few suitable girls' shoes. The difficulty, as I mentioned previously, is that the shoes have to fit over her splints and usually the shop assistants are less than helpful and I direct them with suggestions. This particular assistant is so helpful and thoughtful in making suggestions that it makes the whole experience much less stressful. After an hour or so and trying on so many shoes, we find a pair of boys shoes that fit perfectly as they seem to be wider and more flexible. Dana is not happy at wearing boys' shoes and I wish she didn't have to. At age eleven, Dana is very aware of how she looks to others and just wants to be like any other girl and not be different. I explain why this is necessary and inside I wish she could wear any shoes just because she likes them and not because they are the only ones that fit. This is one of those times when I have to be focused and become emotionally detached. Inside of course, I wish things could be different, but we are here and thinking positively that this is not forever.

The first day of high school brings nervousness on both our parts. I am feeling overprotective, especially knowing how spread out the school is and the number of children attending this school is just under 2000. I can see Dana quite excited by just looking at her; I also see Dana has developed into a strong-minded individual. I still wonder if she will be OK and how will she cope. Quite a few of Dana's junior class are starting high school also, so at least she will have familiar faces with her. Driving into the school again I am reminded at the scale of the school. It is fairly quiet as Dana's year will be the only ones in school in the morning on the first day, as the other years start later that day. Even so there are still over 300 children starting today. Dana's support worker and the head of SENCO meet us and Dana is wheeled to class after being shown to her locker. It is a very strange feeling leaving Dana in high school with a support worker who is a teaching assistant and does not have an understanding of her disability.

As Dana's mother, I have learnt as she has grown, the importance to get a balance between helping her, yet also allowing her to find solutions for problems. We feel it is important for Dana to take responsibility and to propel herself in her wheelchair, not allow others to push her. The school's view is always the amount of time it takes Dana to go from one classroom to another and it is felt for quickness it is better for Dana to be pushed. The amount of children all getting to their classrooms at the same time also causes concern for me. Is Dana able to cope with the high volume of children? Will Dana be ignored and not integrate? Ironically at this time Dana is the only child in a wheelchair – who would have thought out of nearly 2000 children?

Dana starts school in her usual stride. She is so excited and soon meets new friends with whom she had not been at the same junior school with, distancing herself from the friends who were with her during junior years, even the ones who came to her birthday parties. Over the first year of high school it is stressful finding a balance in the approach to take in situations that occur at school and at times, it seems that common sense does not prevail. A cautious approach is adopted by the school, which may be due to a lack of understanding of Dana's disability although I spend time explaining, for example the type of exercises Dana can do in PE with her support worker. PE in my view is an opportunity for Dana to do physiotherapy exercises as she has the support worker allocation. I fought many times to enable Dana to have therapy in school rather than sit in her wheelchair throwing a ball for the entire PE lesson. This is an area I feel so frustrated that Dana's therapy would always be done away from school, meaning time away from lessons. Reports arrive from school stating Dana's attendance will "hopefully improve". How can it improve if she is having therapy outside during school hours? Academically,

Dana is maintaining a good standard and achieving good results. At times it feels the school doesn't fully appreciate the amount of effort and the additional needs Dana has to deal with on top of schooling. I personally feel Dana is coping extremely well. We as parents ensure we work closely with the school, which means as far as Dana is concerned she is able to attend school and feels comfortable without worrying.

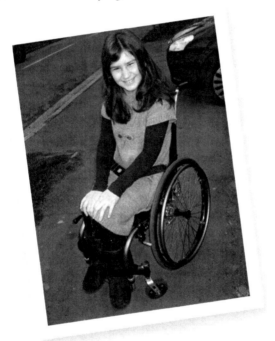

Dana in her wheelchair after a schooling day

In year 8, Dana is nominated for an award. We receive a letter outlining Dana is to be recognised for her academic achievement and inviting us to attend an award ceremony. Attached to the letter is the programme for the evening and among the names of pupils I see Dana's name typed in bold under her year group. This is testament to her determination, personality and the focus she has to her schoolwork. Dana is so excited and can't wait for the ceremony.

As I sit in the school hall with all the other parents waiting for the ceremony to begin, I feel so proud. With everything Dana has to deal with, it proves anything is possible if you set your mind to it. The stage begins to fill with school governors, teachers and of course the head teacher. A large table sits to the left of the stage and is filled with award trophies, all lined in rows. The podium is prepared for the speakers and people are busy ensuring everything is ready for the ceremony. As I look around the school hall, which is full of parents eagerly awaiting the ceremony to begin, most of the parents are holding cameras or phones waiting to capture a picture of their child receiving an award.

I am seated in the stands and have a direct view of the stage and I catch sight of Dana talking happily with her friends. Dana turns round and I catch her eyes and reassure her with a wave and a smile. She looks nervous. As the ceremony begins a short introduction is given to this evening's event and a welcome is extended to the parents. The pupils' names are called one by one in their year groups and they receive their award on the stage, each shaking the school governor's hand and presented with the award. I catch sight of Dana again in the audience with her peers chatting away. It was time for Dana's year group to be called and as each child is called in alphabetical order, they follow each other on stage to receive the awards. The school governor comes to Dana and presents her award as she is sat in her wheelchair and congratulates her. During the award ceremony each year group has a spokesperson who gives a speech on their achievements throughout the school year. It is stated how they have raised funds to help Dana achieve her aim of being out of the wheelchair. This is a very moving moment for me as this shows how Dana's disability has touched teachers and pupils at the school and how highly regarded she is. At that moment all the stress of the previous years in dealing with school issues has disappeared and no longer appears that important. What is important is the tribute to Dana every year group has paid, in front of teachers, pupils and parents. All the teachers speak highly of Dana and this shows she is well liked. She is popular in school and although the school has a very large number of pupils, Dana has settled in quite well. She has a wide circle of friends although she finds talking to boys much easier than talking to girls. I am pleased she is liked and also pleased we have not had to deal with any problems in relation to peer pressure or bullying.

Dana with her school achievement award

Academically my expectation of Dana is to attend university and with this in mind we discuss the subjects to choose for her options. The school arranges an open evening for parents to attend and naturally we would like the opportunity to speak with the teachers and discuss the subjects of interest in more detail. On arrival at the school that evening we are guided to the subjects, which we have discussed with Dana in great length prior to attending. We decide the subjects of interest are Double Science, Spanish, Philosophy, Geography, Maths and English. I am particularly interested in discovering what is covered in Philosophy, as I feel this will increase Dana's confidence and will enable her to start questioning opinions. This is an area that I feel is coupled with the lack of problem solving skills she has not developed. As we discuss the subjects with the teachers it becomes clear Dana is suited to choose these subjects and is given approval to study them.

As Dana progresses through high school it is becoming increasingly more challenging to balance her physiotherapy with schooling. The increase in homework and allowing time for Dana to just relax is something that will always have to be monitored. I often relate the physiotherapy element to a person who is in training for a sport. In order for this person to succeed at a sport, the hours that they train must be a major factor in that person's life. Dana is no different; she must have physiotherapy in her life and, as she grows, she will herself need to find a balance.

Chapter 12

Finding hope for Dana

IN the summer of 2010 and in conversation with friends we find out that their little boy, who also has cerebral palsy has just returned from America following an operation to reduce his spasticity. His parents are so impressed at the improvements in their child's life; I had to find out more about this incredible operation. Why had I not heard about this before? I talked with our friends to find some more information and visit him to see what difference the operation has made. The boy is much younger than Dana and wonder if this would matter. The parents said that they had to raise thousands of pounds for the operation and the rehabilitation after surgery. Clearly this was something which we as Dana's parents had to research thoroughly, as this was a major operation with a high financial and personal cost. The operation called Selective Dorsal Rhizotomy (SDR) is a spinal operation, which dramatically reduces the spasticity in a child who has a specific type of CP.

At Dana's annual hospital appointment with her consultant, I mention to him I had researched SDR and asked if he thought this will benefit Dana. His reply was that his friend does this operation. I sit in the chair amazed at what I am hearing; he knows all about this operation that reduces spasticity for a child, thus improving their independence, why had he not mentioned this as a treatment option for Dana after all these years. His attitude is neither against nor for us continuing in our research, which as you can imagine leaves me quite angry. I am seeking guidance and reassurance that what I am doing is the right thing for Dana and get nothing in return. I know as I sit in the chair in his office, as Dana's mum I will do whatever it takes to make my daughter's life better. No other health professional involved in Dana's care has heard of SDR. I left the consultant's room with Dana clearly knowing I am not going to be supported and feeling alone yet determined to continue with my research.

After several weeks of reading about SDR in great depth and also speaking with other parents of children who had been through this procedure, I decide I have nothing to lose and fill out the application form. The hospital that performs this operation is in America so we do not physically get to see the specialists. The application together with a hip x-ray, spinal x-ray, MRI scan and video footage of preset movements of Dana, are sent to the hospital. A panel will review everything and make a decision on whether Dana is a suitable candidate for the operation. Days turn into weeks and it feels the wait is taking forever. My thoughts turn to what Dana's life will be like if she is accepted and then I also think what life will be like if she is rejected. The waiting is the most stressful; waiting to hear; this is out of my hands, I have no control over the decision, and it will be a yes or no.

On the 22nd November 2010 in my inbox amongst the other email messages, there it sat, the decision from the hospital confirming if Dana is a suitable candidate for the operation. I feel a sense of nervousness rushing through my body and I am too scared to open the email and read it. I am preparing myself for bad news and good news, hoping I will not have to deal with the bad news. Sitting staring at the screen, which seems like ages, I take a depth breath and open the email. There it is 'Congratulations' that is enough for me to read and leap in the air with joy. Yes, Dana has been accepted and I settle down to read the email properly. As I continue reading the email, it confirms how Dana will benefit from having SDR. Dana will walk in protected environments unaided and in all other environments with sticks. This is incredible reading.

Later that day I give Dana the good news and discuss possible dates for the operation, bearing in mind there is a lot of money to raise. The hospital has given me an estimated cost for the operation, post op physiotherapy, equipment if applicable and orthopaedic procedures. I also added to this the cost of private physiotherapy as part of Dana's rehabilitation when we returned home. Costing everything altogether our target is £60,000. My feeling is I aim to fundraise to fund this procedure and the rehabilitation and only want to do this the once. So many families I had spoken with had fundraised only to cover for the operation and when they returned home they had to continue fundraising for the continuing rehabilitation. My approach is to focus my attention on Dana when we return home. Although the news is fantastic, I am also mourning the loss of my mum, Dana's nanny at the same time. I have a funeral to arrange and unable to cope with starting something that I know I am unable to focus on 100%. We decide to wait until the New Year to start fundraising.

The operation in America has been set for the 4th August 2011, and so I begin researching the internet to attain knowledge of fundraising. I have no knowledge of where to begin and speak with other parents who had already been through this stage. With our target of £60,000 by August, I wasn't sure how we would achieve this; all I did know was that we will reach this figure. Others around me are not so confident, which caused upset. There is a lot of negativity surrounding me, and so it is important for me to be focused. I know I have to acquire the funds as Dana not having the operation is definitely not an option. I will never allow that to happen.

I begin by contacting local media as they are important in not only raising Dana's fundraising profile but to keep the interest amongst the fundraising activities we arrange. Alongside this we open a community account with a bank to hold the fund that is raised. Just with these in place it is very unfamiliar to me and I have to start thinking differently. How am I going to attract people to know about Dana's appeal and raise the profile enough to compete with all the other fundraising causes? We set up Dana's charity name as *Dana's Walk to the Stars* and suddenly the focus is on a cause. Yes, it is about Dana, but the focus is about raising enough funds for an operation that will dramatically change a girl's life forever. We have a short time frame to do this and I have to dedicate all my time and effort in achieving the end result. I have a website designed, which gives a good description of who we are as a family, Dana's disability, what the operation is, a list of fundraising activities, a blog, contact details, and a gauge showing funds raised so far. The website allows me to link into social media groups, which is something I have no previous knowledge of. It all feels very alien at first but I have to get used to how this works very quickly and most importantly how these sites can help Dana's appeal. Using some of the fundraising ideas that had been successful for other parents I start to list some ideas and possible venues. I come out of my comfort zone and start approaching companies face to face armed with publicity material.

It does feel like begging at first, but this is not about me, it is about Dana. By this stage we have been featured in the papers and I have posters made of Dana's appeal and part of the publicity folder I carry around with me promoting the charity. I learn very quickly the approach to take for different companies depending on the size and independence of the organisation. The rejection is the hardest part, as for me it feels they are rejecting in helping Dana, although for some it is company policy. Thankfully these rejections are few. I write to the major organisations asking for their support in ways, which they feel, will be most suitable for them and I am grateful for the generous responses received. The fundraising is starting to gain pace and to keep track of everything and take control, I buy a whiteboard and pin board. At the end of each day I update the whiteboard with a list of things to do and when the activities have been planned for. Receipts and contact details are pinned to the board.

Dana with Oliver at one of the fundraising events, a 1950s dinner and dance

It is starting to be a full-time job and I have to be on top of everything. I feel the charity is missing a marketing angle and search the internet on marketing ideas. I want items that complement the events already planned and also that people can buy and promote Dana's charity. Wristbands seem to be the most popular and I design one with a company a logo and colour for Dana's charity. As the name was Dana's *Walk to the Stars*, I choose six stars at the end of the name, the web address and blue and red as the colours. These are so popular I have to repeat my original order as they have sold so well. I also ordered key rings and these are sold particularly at larger fundraising events. I am being approached by strangers, from children to adults who want to be sponsored and take this upon themselves to organise. We are receiving donations from strangers in the post. It is incredible how people are willing to do this act of kindness for someone they do not know. For all the charity events I supply tee shirts that I designed with Dana's appeal details together with charity money buckets and sponsorship forms. Suddenly I am not able to keep control of all the events as there are so many being run but I always have an overview of who is doing what and where.

The weeks seem to fly by as we either are organizing the events ourselves or we attend events organised by others. It is important for Dana to be present and to talk with other people. We went from attending military assault courses to events run in pubs. Local shops have collection tins and it is important for Dana to visit these and meet the customers. Schools run mufti days, and children, teachers and parents give so generously. I run a fun day at a shopping centre and with the support of the centre manager arrange activities throughout the whole three floors of the shopping centre. We have face painting, portrait sketchers, craft stalls, a talent show and some of the shops have their own activities arranged as part of the day. There are always plenty of volunteers who wear their charity T-shirts, who stand with collection buckets, while others help with various activities. A tall banner stands at the entrance of the shopping centre, which is a larger version of the appeal poster and people read about Dana and why we are fundraising. As parents we explain in great detail how their money will help to change Dana's life forever. It is such an exhausting day yet rewarding, not just because we are fundraising, but to see all the community come together to help someone lead an independent life.

We contact all the supermarkets to request permission to bag pack; some more forthcoming than others. One particular supermarket stands out as they make us feel very welcome and the staff are very friendly. We return a few times and the staff always ask how the fundraising is going and how Dana is feeling. I remember the first time we bag packed, a number of volunteers arriving at the supermarket at 9am, I gave each a tee shirt to wear and a collection bucket. Each person stood at a till point and helped the customers pack their bags. At one point I looked at all the till points and saw my volunteers in their tee shirts and in front of them Dana's appeal poster and pink charity buckets and I felt very honoured and privileged I had so many people give up their time to help Dana.

It is amazing at the creativity people have in suggestions for fundraising events. A gym hold a fitness weekend, which have different type of classes running and people pay an entrance fee to join in. I am contacted by someone who wants to run from Sparta to Athens and would like to fundraise for Dana, which was unimaginable for me. I am always grateful and overwhelmed at the kindness people have shown.

In addition to the events, I ensure the website reflects events in real time. All the publicity has to be up-to-date and as an event takes place and funds are counted, I ensure the amounts are on the website. It is important for everyone to see how we are raising the funds and also for people who are following our journey to share our experience with us. The events are building up fast and we hold between four to five events a month and this continues for over five months. This coupled with having to go to work, Dana and my son going to school and running a home, the stress levels as you can imagine are starting to rise. Tensions are running high at home and I am getting close to breaking point. Although I have made some great friendships to keep my spirits up, it still feels very much I am alone in my aim to succeed as others expect me to fail. Close friends who I thought I could count on, refuse to help and some family are less than helpful, which really hurts deeply. Complete strangers who do not know Dana are giving up their time and doing things to help, yet some close friends and some family are simply not willing to support us. Although this hurts deeply, in the scheme of things it is not important and my focus is on raising funds not thinking about why people do not want to help. I can't change other people; I can only change myself.

It is July 2011, not only have we reached our target of £60,000, we have in fact exceeded this and raised an incredible total amount of £75,000. It is such an overwhelming feeling how after such an enormous amount of hard work and stressful periods, this amazing figure is reached. I am relieved and also my sanity is intact. No amounts of words can ever express how truly grateful I feel at people's selfless acts. Dana can and will begin a new life on 4th August 2011.

Chapter 13

→ ←

The trip that changes Dana's life forever

THE hospital in the USA contact me to advise that they require a deposit before we fly for Dana's surgery and I arrange with the bank, which holds Dana's funds to wire transfer the required amount of money. Sitting in an office at the bank I read out the hospital bank details, making sure the service agent types in the correct information into the computer. The agent must have thought I was pushy but I knew everything had to be right; there was a lot at stake if the hospital fails to receive the deposit.

Within days the deposit has been received by the hospital and that is the last action I have to take before our departure to the USA. Dana is breaking up from school for the summer shortly and all our attention is focused on the trip and of course the operation. Making sure Dana keeps healthy is a priority and I keep her away from anyone who even looks like they have a cold. I am a tad over cautious, yet I do what I have to do.

I look at the letter again from the hospital, "will walk unaided in protected environments and with crutches in outside environments". This is the prognosis given by the panel at the hospital who have confirmed Dana is a suitable candidate for SDR. I read this over and over again and feel a sense of excitement at the future, which by today's standard is very different. Dana is in her wheelchair 90% of the time and uses a walking frame at home. This operation is truly life changing. Little did I know, this is the procedure that I have been searching for all these years and I find it by pure chance. It saddens me no one in the health profession has come across this other than of course Dana's consultant, who I am not sure why in all the years Dana has been in his care this has never been a treatment option open for discussion. Still, that is all in the past, which I am unable to change, I need to look at the future and be grateful we are at this point. Dana has the final say whether to have the operation. At thirteen years of age, Dana has the right to decide how she wishes to live her life.

The flight is booked for July 29th 2011 giving us a few days to get over the journey and settle in before the operation date. Two flight tickets have been generously donated by an airline and I arrange with the relevant department the flight details. It is all starting to feel very surreal. We are travelling to the USA for an operation. I hadn't known anyone who had operations abroad before and I am taking my daughter to America. I know Dana is in safe hands as the chief neurosurgeon is considered one of the top doctors in America and he has performed over 2000 operations on other children and adults. Selective Dorsal Rhizotomy (SDR) is unique as it reduces or completely eliminates spasticity in children who have a specific CP. Over the past twenty years this technique has been refined and the procedure involves removing one vertebra in the spine. The neurosurgeon divides each of the dorsal roots into three to five rootlets and stimulates each rootlet electrically; the surgical team identifies the rootlets that cause spasticity. The abnormal rootlets are selectively cut, leaving the normal rootlets intact. The surgical procedure takes between two and a half, to three and a half hours in total, depending on the child's age. The older the child, then the longer the procedure. The incision is then glued together rather than stitched and covered with a dressing.

I watched a programme where a TV crew had travelled to America with a family whose son was having SDR and they also filmed the operation. I sit with Dana the second time and we watch the operation together. Dana wants to see what to expect and is remarkably calm. I on the other hand feel even more nervous. Dana is very mature and asks so many questions, some of which I do not have the answers to. So, Dana makes contact with the boy who was on TV and asks questions specifically about how it felt having the operation.

I am packing for a trip aboard but it's not a holiday. My nerves are starting to show and I guess a bit of fear – is this right for Dana? Of course I know it is. I have a file with the letters from the hospital, flight details, hotel details, copies of the money transfers and every-thing to do with the operation. It feels more like a business trip and to keep my mind focused it helps to be thinking this way. Staying away from home for five weeks means that not only is the packing for every day, but I have to also pack for the days Dana is in hospital and for discharge. I am conscious that I pack clothes that are loose, nothing tight and difficult to take off. I will lay Dana's flight clothes out on her bed the night before so everything runs smoothly in the morning. I am unable to sleep at all the night before, my mind is racing around thinking of what to expect over the next five weeks. I have prepared Dana as much as I can and prepared myself also. Nothing though prepares you for living the experience. We have an early flight from London Heathrow and a people-carrier taxi drives us to the airport. We have four suitcases, a walking frame, hand luggage and a wheelchair and are thankful when we check in the items at the airport.

Our flight to New York takes just under eight hours. Once we arrive and claim our baggage, we find our connecting flight to our final destination, St Louis and board a transit train to another ter-minal. Again we check in our baggage and make our way to the gate, ready to board our internal flight. Outside the rain is increasing and a storm is developing, our flight to St Louis has been delayed. Looking around there are no ground staff to be seen and I end up calling reservations from an airport phone to speak to someone. My nerves are already shattered and I stand in the middle of the airport crying. I feel so alone, no one is helping – I have to get Dana to St Louis but all the planes have stopped landing and taking off from New York. All I can do is sit and wait. The time seems to stand still, looking out of the window the weather is not easing. People are increasing as they come and sit by their gates, waiting for news of when their flights are ready to board.

Several hours later, we are finally called to board, and by this time, it is 9pm, New York time. It is a few hours flight to St Louis and we all are extremely tired. Boarding the plane, which only has eighteen rows and three seats across, our seats are midway. As I step in the aircraft it feels rather cramped as earlier we had been on much larger plane; looking to my left there is the cockpit and to my right the seating. There is one steward on board and the plane soon fills with all the passengers. I am feeling very apprehensive about the flight and I am a confident flyer. I say a prayer as the steward prepares for take-off. Most of the passengers sleep during the flight; even the steward sits in the back row. I am too conscious of all the noises the plane is making to sleep and just wishing we could land in St Louis soon.

After travelling for 24 hours we finally arrive at our hotel, our home for the next five weeks. We are all exhausted and just want our beds. As we check in we are given an envelope, as we are welcomed to St Louis. The envelope is an information pack from the hospital. This is certainly something I am not able to read until the morning, and the only thing we are doing is going to sleep.

During the first few days in St Louis we start to meet families whose children had been through SDR. We are in this new environment where everything seems unfamiliar and the operation date is firmly on my mind. A reassurance from other families does not ease my anxieties, although I know it is done with the best intentions. Seeing the children walk around literally after a few weeks following major surgery is incredible and unbelievable. The children laughing with other children, all strangers to one other at the start of their journeys are now bonded by an experience which others will never understand. Parents are talking to each other, again a bond grows from total strangers to becoming friends as they share the low times and the good times. All the parents of post SDR children understand my nervousness as they were all in my situation once and talk me through what to expect. Dana sits and listens. The other children are quite young, much younger than Dana, so she is unable to sit and have a discussion and ask them questions. The only feedback is from parents, which is fine for me, but I am not going through the operation. Dana asks questions about the hospital; she is not unfamiliar with hospitals in the UK so has this image to measure against. They tell Dana she is able to choose her own flavoured anaesthetic; Dana asks if they have chocolate flavour.

One of the last pictures taken as a family on holiday before SDR

We keep the weekend as normal as possible, going grocery shopping as our apartment in the hotel has a fitted kitchen so we are able to make it a home from home. The facilities within the hotel allow us to be flexible with the option of choosing to have breakfast provided by the hotel or not. The staff are mindful that we and other families are staying for five weeks and they cannot do enough for us. The hotel run a regular shuttle bus service within a three-mile radius and the children's hospital is a regular stop. The drivers get to know the families really well and become part of their lives, asking after the children's well-being and generally getting to know each family. It is incredible to witness; this is not just a hotel but also a sense of community, families come and feel safe together and share this very important time in their children's lives.

It is Monday morning and the day we meet the doctor who will change Dana's life forever. Dr Park of St Louis Children's Hospital, chief neurosurgeon is considered to be one of the top doctors in the USA, and on Thursday 4th August he will perform SDR on Dana. Today we are meeting Dr Park and he will evaluate Dana and hopefully still agree the operation will be as successful as he has stated. Sitting in the waiting room with another family whose son is also having the same operation, we are all nervously waiting to be called in. The other family is called in first and I look around and stare at the many pictures on the wall and take in just how colourful the hospital is. I think back about when I walked into the hospital and was greeted by the most cheerful security guard I have ever met, who will become a familiar face to us over the next five weeks. He directs us to where we need to go and wishes us well for our appointment. He is a very humble man with the most wonderful smile. He greets each and every person with a good morning and a time check, while still maintaining our attention. Back in the waiting room, my thoughts are interrupted; it is our turn and we are shown to a little room, and we sit down and watch a short DVD explaining what SDR is and facts about spasticity. I get a sinking feeling in my stomach even though we had seen the operation on TV many times and researched the procedure. This is different as it is actually going to happen to Dana. I pinch myself as I think how fortunate we are Dana has been given this opportunity and terrified at the same time we are putting Dana through this operation. The alternative, which is to do nothing, is not an option. Dana would spend the rest of her life wheelchair bound and I was not going to let that happen. Health professionals in the UK, I feel have given up on Dana. I never have, and always knew there was a treatment which would benefit Dana and allow her to lead the life she deserves.

The DVD lasts a very short time and we are then shown to another room where Dr Park will join us in a little while. Sitting on the sofa, I cannot keep still. I feel I am waiting for a VIP to walk in. I am extremely nervous, my hands are sweating and I sit on the edge of the seat. Dana is very quiet, what is she thinking? She smiled and said she feels OK, yet understandably she is nervous. The door opens and Dr Park and a colleague walk in and immediately shake our hands. I sit down again on the edge of the seat and hang on his every word, desperately trying to remember everything he is saying. He evaluates Dana and confirms Dana will walk unaided in pro- tected environments and with crutches outside. He continues and discusses how the spasticity has affected Dana's body over the years. Spasticity has no benefit; it has caused many deformities in Dana, as her body has had to adjust to compensate for the lack of movement. My joy fills with tears as the thought of Dana's future is beginning to actually become a reality. My thought also turned to thinking if only, if only Dana had SDR when she was much younger, before any deformities developed. I felt jealous at the younger children back at the hotel for a moment, then happiness. Happiness they will never have the deformities Dana has and happiness they are young enough to not know any different as they get older. Dana's rehabilitation following the operation will take two years. What is two years of her life as she is only thirteen years old? Dana may also need some orthopaedic surgery and we will have this confirmed when we see the orthopaedic surgeon. We are expecting this as Dana's right side is worse affected. The operation set for Thursday is confirmed and we are given paperwork that outlines the process to follow in preparation for surgery day.

In the x-ray department, waiting to be called for our appointment

The next two days we return for further pre surgery evaluations, this time with one of the physiotherapists who also films Dana as she moves around the floor and attempts to climb up and down the stairs. This is to understand what Dana is able or unable to do, and also to measure her range of movement. The final stage in the pre surgical procedures is a visit to the X-ray department to mark on Dana's back where Dr Park will make the incision on Thursday. Arriving at the X-ray department we are met by a clown, and a magician who entertain the children as they wait for their appointments. One of the magicians starts to perform a trick and all the children become involved. For a moment you actually forget where you are and can be forgiven for enjoying the entertainment. Dana is called and we follow the nurse to the X-ray room. I am helped lifting Dana on to the bed and then handed a protective heavy apron by a nurse. We start to chat about the Royal Wedding as three doctors arrive, each of them shaking my hand and introducing themselves. With Dana's back exposed, the X-ray machine is placed over her back and the light shines on her lower spine. A pair of metal scissors is laid flat on the spot where the incision will be made, and the X-ray is taken. One of the doctors is handed a black marker and places an X on Dana's lower spine to mark the spot. The doctors wish Dana and I all the very best and say goodbye. With a respectful manner and endearing approach, I am overwhelmed to witness such genuine concern. As I push Dana in her wheelchair out of the department, my thoughts turn to Thursday – operation day.

Chapter 14

⇥ ⇤

The operation

I hardly sleep all night and see the sky turn from dark to light. It's Thursday morning and today is operation day. Dana is first on the theatre list, which I'm pleased about, as she should be in recovery by lunchtime. Waking Dana up from the deep sleep she is in, to allow sufficient time to get to the hospital, I am met with a groan and a firm statement of "I don't want to go". I reassure Dana as she slowly wakes that everything will be OK, this is the worst bit and it's natural to feel nervous not knowing what to expect. Deep down I am petrified and continue to maintain an outer positive attitude. At this point Dana is crying begging me not to make her go through with the operation. This is so hard as I wish I didn't have to make her go through with this and ultimately wish she wasn't disabled; however, I know deep down this is the right procedure. We had spent months researching this operation, speaking with other parents, sending all the pre evaluation information to the hospital in America and the panel agreed Dana is a suitable candidate and outlined the benefits gained from this operation. This is going to change Dana and our lives forever. Dana will always be disabled and the operation is not a miracle cure, I know that. The disability has made Dana who she is today and if she was not disabled she would not be Dana. SDR will give her a life without spasticity. A life where her body can move more freely and not develop further deformities.

I was instructed by the hospital staff the day before to arrive at the hospital by 5.45am, as Dana is due in theatre at 7.30am, so I ensure a taxi is booked to collect us from the hotel at 5.15am Dana and I wait in the hotel lobby, the lights are dim and staff arrive to start their working day and greet us as they walk in. Soft music is playing quietly and I try to listen and gain some distraction from the nervousness I am feeling. Looking at the large clock hanging above the fireplace it is 5.15 and still no taxi. As you can imagine I am starting to feel panicky, Dana is getting upset and I am doing my best to calm her while I am also trying to remain calm. Fortunately the front desk is manned 24hrs a day and the receptionist is able to make contact with the owner of the taxi firm. Apparently the driver has overslept and is too far away, therefore the owner of the taxi company is going to come and take us to the hospital. By the time he arrives it is 5.30am and we have fifteen minutes to arrive at the hospital. My nerves are shattered, it takes all my strength not to burst into tears. The journey to the hospital is short and filled with reassuring Dana. We arrive at the front entrance of the hospital and I take a deep breath as I push Dana in her wheelchair to the doors, pulling a small suitcase behind me. This is it, the biggest decision we all as a family had been planning for. Ultimately the final decision lay with Dana, as parents we felt at thirteen years of age, she was old enough to decide how she wished her future to be. We would support Dana whatever she decided.

The friendly security guard had yet to start work and for a hospital it was very quiet and looked very empty. How I missed his reassuring smile and well-chosen words of comfort. Heading towards the lift I look and confirm the floor that Dana needs to register. As the lift doors opened we walk into a very noisy and busy floor. There are certainly lots of children who are having procedures done this morning. As we walk toward reception to register Dana's arrival, we pass several hubs filled with sofas and televisions, family members waiting for news of their own children's procedures. The family name is written on the outside of each of the hubs. I wonder if we will be allocated one to sit in during Dana's operation. Other families are sitting in rows in a large waiting room, where they help themselves to complimentary coffee. Certainly very different from what we had experienced in the UK. Greeted by the receptionist, who takes down Dana's details, she advises we have an allocated room to wait in while Dana is in theatre. She called it the VIP room as all Dr Park's patients receive this treatment. Again I know that Dana is in good hands. As the receptionist is talking I glance behind and there is the room, door shut and Dana's name written on the white board. It suddenly becomes very real again, the reason why we had woken up so early and why we are in a hospital. I feel nervous again as the receptionist concludes and advises us to take a seat in the allocated room and a nurse will be with us shortly.

Dana and I sit together alone in the room. Switching the television on to get some distraction from what was happening, Dana sits quietly and occasionally saying firmly she cannot go through with the operation. I keep reassuring her and talking about what she will be able to do once she has recovered from the operation. It is important Dana thinks of the future and looks at how different her life will be. I didn't know how, myself, but I did know there would no longer be a wheelchair and that for me, and Dana is a good starting point.

A nurse suddenly appears in our room and calls for Dana to be taken to the pre-med cubicle. I take my usual deep breaths as I push Dana into a room, which is equipped as expected. A gown is brought for Dana to change into and a stream of health professionals come in to speak to us one after the other. Their mannerisms are very professional each introducing themselves and explain in detail the purpose of their roles in caring for Dana. Not one person takes for granted that another person has told me something. Dana is extremely nervous at this point and it shows, her body is shaking and she still keeps saying she can't go through with the operation. The nurse comes back and forth into the room and on one of the occasions, she brings Dana's pre-med. Now in the past Dana does not cope very well with two things when in hospital; needles and pre-meds. I knew I was going to have difficulty and sure enough when the nurse gives a small cupful of medicine, Dana refuses to take it, shutting her lips tightly. I request the nurse put the pre-med in a syringe and have a small glass of apple juice ready for afterwards. The nurse hands me the syringe and lets me administer the pre-med to Dana. Dana resists me every bit and I have to speak firmly to her and put the syringe in the side of her mouth, followed quickly by the apple juice. Dana keeps retching and I keep firm by calmly asking her to swallow. The apple juice is spat over me, which in the scheme of things is a very small price to pay.

Everyone explains to Dana in fine detail exactly what each step will be and she equally is asking lots of questions. I am comforted that Dana is able to speak openly, as for any child in the same situation, undergoing a major operation is dramatic enough. To have a doctor and his team in America, who Dana has only recently met, perform the operation is just overwhelming. I am incredibly proud of how courageous Dana has been and she has shown great strength in her ability to overcome her fears and anxieties.

I look at the clock on the wall and time is moving quickly, soon it will be time for Dana to be taken to theatre. I am grateful the pre-med has taken affect now and Dana is lying in the hospital gown drowsy and talking nonsense. A child's play specialist has been called to visit Dana prior to surgery, as they felt she was quite anxious and by the time he has arrived, Dana is feeling rather relaxed. She does, however, manage to use his iPad and starts talking about the Royal Wedding. The consideration given to Dana's well-being goes further than just medically and the holistic side is equally as important. Suddenly the room is filled with nurses; it is time for Dana to be taken down to theatre. I feel sick. I walk beside her as she is wheeled on the bed to theatre and we stop at end of the corridor. I stroke Dana's head and inform her that I will see her later and the nurses wheel her away from me. I stand frozen on the spot, tears streaming down my face as I watch the bed turn a corner and she is gone. I turn round to head out towards the room that has been allocated for us to wait in and I can't seem to get my bearings. I feel so disoriented. Nurses are busy walking around and I feel I am not in that moment. I am physically shown the right direction to go and soon find the familiar room. Dana's wheelchair is now sitting empty, and her clothes are lying on the chair. It just feels so lonely. I know Dana is in safe hands and how much more independence she will have. I keep reaffirming these words in my mind.

An hour has passed and the phone call from theatre, which had been mentioned, has not occurred. Was there something wrong? Was the telephone working? Had the staff forgotten? I spoke to reception and asked if they had heard anything, who reassures me everything is fine. Still this does not reassure me and with sweaty palms and shaking hands I go back to the room and wait. I look at the phone and pick it up to make sure it is working. A few moments later the phone rings, a ring so loud, it is unmistakable to not hear it. The voice on the other end of the phone said the operation had commenced fifteen minutes ago and everything is going fine. Dana had been sedated successfully. What a relief and attempt to relax before our next phone call update. I see a family who are due to go home to the UK today and they are saying their goodbyes to the hospital staff. The grandmother of the boy, who had the surgery five weeks ago comes into the room to wish us well and gives me a cuddle. We both start to cry, I was feeling scared as the operation is at the midway point, not knowing what to expect, and the grand-mother understands how I am feeling and reassures me everything is going to be alright. I seek comfort from speaking with people on a social media forum who all had been in the same room as I am right now. All have experienced the same feelings and all know what and when to say. Although most are from the UK, others are from all over the world, yet we speak, all united by this operation and our children.

The phone rings again; it is our update from theatre. All went well and they are just closing Dana up and the surgeon will be with us shortly. Within minutes Dr Park glides into the room. I stand up instantly and he said: "Everything went fine." I hang on his every word and long for him to say more; he was pleased how the operation went and left as gently as he had entered. We will get another call when Dana has been transferred to recovery and we are able to see her. It has been the longest time of my life and I am so relieved I will be seeing Dana very soon.

Walking to the recovery area I wonder how Dana is feeling and how she will look, after all she has just had a spinal operation, which lasted just over three hours and I cannot imagine how I will find her. The nurses point me to bed 13 where they have placed Dana. Bed 13, "great", I think, as I walk in search of Dana. Why could she not have been in bed 12 or bed 14? Is this a sign of how bad things will be? I am faced with bed 13 directly in front of me, and I can see Dana's body lying flat and I sheepishly walk towards her. She is wired to machines that continue to bleep as a nurse is controlling her pain relief. I introduce myself to the nurse who looks at my shocked face. She assures me Dana is doing really well and shortly will be transferred to intensive care. Dana is calling "mummy it hurts" and I stroke her swollen face. Her eyes and lips look quite scary, too. The nurse said that this is typical after this type of surgery, as Dana has been face-down in theatre for a number of hours. I talk to Dana to reassure her that I am with her now and the operation is all over and she is such a brave girl. Inside I was crying at how Dana looked, as this is shocking and upsetting and if totally honest I am worried that the swelling will not go down. Within the hour we are making our way to intensive care. All our things have been cleared from the 'VIP' room and I follow the nurse to intensive care, thinking another family will go through the same feelings as I had just been through today and imagining what child will be operated on next. Every bump the bed went over as Dana is wheeled she feels and moans in pain. All I can do is hold her hand as she has been given enough pain relief to see her to intensive care.

Intensive care is made up of individual cubicles that are staffed with a ratio of one nurse for every three patients. There is a communal room that is divided into a kitchenette with seating and an area for parents to sleep. It is all very strange learning where everything is and as a parent what to do. I have to wait until Dana is settled into her cubicle as she has IV lines and has to be attached to the monitor. As I wait in the parents' area, other parents come in, some still in their pyjamas getting a drink, others are resting in the makeshift beds. I notice one parent sitting talking on the phone crying as she is talking about her child who is still in intensive care. Seeing this increases my anxieties and I know Dana has to remain here for 24 hrs minimum, hoping there are no complications overnight. A nurse calls me through as Dana is settling in.

Mickey, who is a young bubbly intensive care nurse, introduces herself, as she will be looking after Dana. She explains the medication Dana has been given and mentions the catheter will be removed before Dana is transferred to the ward. I am still concerned with the swelling on Dana's face and she said this is usual for the next few days. She hands me a bag, which contains essential items for an overnight stay, information about the hospital and a map of the hospital. I am allowed to stay overnight with Dana in the intensive care room with a chair converting into a bed. Not only do the staff ensure Dana is cared for, but they also make sure I am OK and regularly ask if there is anything I require. The care and attention to detail far exceeds my expectations and I have never experienced such kindness and professionalism from health professionals. The surgeon comes to visit Dana ensuring all is well. He checks her toes and looks at her legs, and again, these are also swollen, which like her face is to be expected. Dana is clearly under the influence of morphine as she tells the surgeon *to be careful when touching her leg as she had just had an operation.* The surgeon smiles to himself and said Dana is doing well. Later that day I would go to the hospital library as patients are able to borrow DVDs to watch as each intensive care room has its own television and DVD player, and to borrow a couple of films which Dana likes. I play one of the films and sit next to Dana in the chair watching the film together. Within minutes Dana is asleep and I just let the film run. Mickey comes in and asks if everything is OK. "She's asleep," I say and she walks out with a smile. Dana is kept lying flat in bed for the next few days and is only allowed to take sips of water. She is craving for food and it is so hard to say no. I do give Dana some cream crackers by the evening, breaking them in tiny pieces so she doesn't choke. Every few hours Dana complains of pain in her back, so Mickey comes and checks her medication and administers another type to ease the pain. Dana is getting spasms now, which are the nerves in her back. The medication given will ease the pain. Nothing passes Dana and she insists on knowing what the nurse is doing and what medication she is being given. Dana is also still fretful the IV line is still in her hand and wants this removed immediately. Mickey and I both explain to her that it is to allow the medication to work much more quickly. I know she absolutely dislikes needles and requests for her hand to be bandaged so she does not see the needle.

As I convert the chair into my bed for the night, I hope Dana has a restful and peaceful sleep, yet I suspect this is not going to be the case. I prepare myself for bed and ensure Dana is comfortable, while the nurse checks her vital signs as usual and ensures she is pain free for the moment. The night is one of the longest and hardest, as Dana wakes every few hours screaming in pain. I am up every time Dana screams, pressing the buzzer for the nurse, which is an intercom, waiting to speak and tell the nurse what I need. This is repetitive through the night and I am grateful when I look out of the window and see sunrise. Thank goodness it is morning.

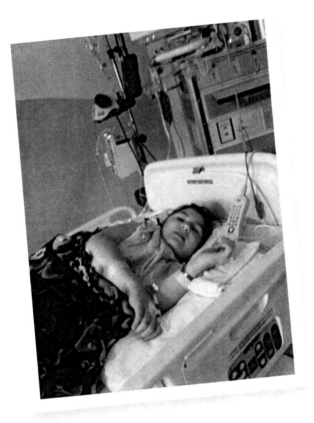

Attached to a monitor and lines in intensive care

Chapter 15

Rehabilitation

MOVING to the ward is a major milestone, as not only is Dana recovering as expected, we are one step forward to commencing physiotherapy. Once settled in, the ward consists of rooms with two beds and is spacious enough to feel like two rooms. Each bed has a TV and DVD, along with the familiar chair that converts to a bed and a wardrobe. A bathroom is also in the room. It feels more like a hotel room than a hospital room. A whiteboard faces Dana's bed that has the names of the doctors and nurses who are looking after Dana and the plan for the day. Sometimes the nurses will leave messages such as *sleep well* with a smiley face. It may appear a minor gesture, yet it means a great deal knowing the staff generally care for your child's well-being.

The time on the ward is filled with a mixture of emotions, tears, joy and laughter. Pain relief is maintained at a high level not allowing Dana to be in discomfort. During the day, every few hours Dana is turned from side to side and eventually is also allowed to sit elevated. I stock up on a selection of DVDs for Dana to watch and keep her entertained. However, her favourite pastime is to chat with her friends on Facebook, which allows her to at least talk to some familiar faces and adds normality to her day. As soon as the antibiotics finish in the morning, Dana has the option of the IVs coming out. There are two conditions; one, Dana increases her fluids and two, she is able to take oral Valium. Dana agrees to both and the nurse, Allie, takes the IVs out a day ahead of schedule.

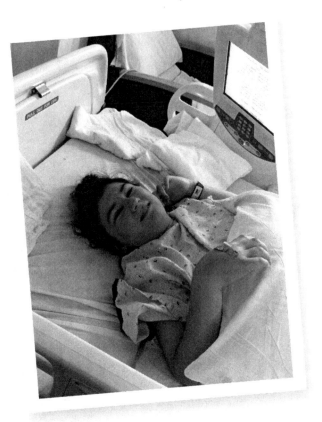

On the ward watching TV

Dana seems to be repeating herself; I'm thinking it's the meds as she definitely was not like this pre op. She has stages when she is pain free yet other times when the pain hits, she screams in agony. Allie is great at calming Dana down and talking through what meds she has given her. I start changing Dana and get told that I'm not a professional and that I should leave it for Allie. Allie laughs and said; "Your mom has done a pretty good job these last thirteen years." Dana's reply is: "No, she's done a terrible job these last thirteen years." With my mouth wide open in shock at what Dana has just said, I let it go as again it's the meds talking. I carry on helping Allie change Dana and get her comfy again.

Later in the day Dr Park visits Dana and asks how she is feeling as he is looking at her feet. She says fine and as Dr Park asks about her legs Dana says: "Be careful, my legs are attached to my spine." I look up at Dr Park who is laughing as is another doctor standing next to him.

Day three sees Dana out of bed for the first time and the first physiotherapy session. The day is centred on this and the pain relief is timed accordingly. It is an extremely important day that also brings a sense of anxiety for both Dana and I, knowing that only three days ago she underwent major spinal surgery and is now preparing to get out of bed and start physiotherapy. The therapist arrives, explains how slowly the first day will be dividing her time between the morning and the afternoon. I assist the therapist with slowly moving Dana's legs to the side of the bed in order to stand her upright. Immediately Dana is sick, twice. How can she have therapy as she is unable to stand without being sick? My frustration shows and I am reassured this is completely normal. When Dana feels ready to stand, the therapist and I both assist and she is able to stand for a few moments. This shows great courage and determination from Dana as I am sure she is feeling scared and unsure of what to expect. Her pain levels are maintained although at this stage I am not sure if she is feeling anxious and therefore is saying it is painful. Her body of course must feel different to the tightness felt before surgery. This is a new experience for her and it is going to take some time to get used to her new body. The morning physiotherapy session is aimed at answering lots of questions from us as parents and getting Dana out of her bed, while in the afternoon the physiotherapist is tasked with getting Dana into her wheelchair. The technique we are shown is specifically supporting Dana whilst transferring from the bed to the wheelchair. She holds the therapist's neck tightly as he moves her body and again looks anxious. The transfer looks easy, however, when we attempt the same manoeuvre, we struggle greatly. Is it the way we held her or could Dana feel our apprehension? We knew we had to get it right as once Dana is discharged from hospital in two days time and back at the hotel, we are on our own. We are advised for Dana to rest a while and then repeat the transfer from the bed to wheelchair later that afternoon. We were on our own and felt rather in the deep end of a swimming pool – it's sink or swim!!

Dana rested and watched a DVD, the morning and afternoon physiotherapy really did take its toll on her, which is as expected. Later in the afternoon, as instructed we attempt to transfer Dana from bed to wheelchair with the aim of taking her to the cafeteria for a change of scenery. After the third attempt we successfully achieve this leaving us exhausted. We are conscious of the scar on her back and ensure Dana is reassured we are not going to touch it. My thought turns to thinking about repeating the process in reverse and all the forthcoming days. It's not something I am relishing.

Before attempting to transfer Dana, we adopt a step-by-step plan and run through how the transfer would take place. The wheelchair is placed in the correct position and Dana is seated on the edge of the bed. A run through of transfer would take place several times before we actually attempt to transfer Dana. Day four Dana continues with very gentle physiotherapy and we take her down to the therapy department twice during the day.

By the time day five arrives, Dana is ready to be discharged. The doctors are around to ensure she is fit to leave and the nurses arrange for the medication to be picked up from the pharmacy on our way out. The doctors feel her legs and ask how she is feeling.

"My legs feel divorced," she replies. What a great description and above all, a very mature reply. For me, I finally understand what it must have been like for Dana living with the spasticity. How tight must her legs have been? To be able to move each leg separately from each other on command is such a simple task for most of us, yet a mammoth achievement for Dana. I think back to Dana's younger years and wonder if her legs felt as tight back then to the years that have followed. One thing that hurts me is knowing what I know now; I always did the optimum for Dana. On the one hand I feel I let her down, on the other, it has made me a stronger person and Dana certainly would not be the caring, approachable and mature person she is today. I am still learning today and will continue to do so as Dana begins a new journey – a new life.

Stocked up with two bags full of medication, discharge papers, get well cards and balloons; we make our way out of the hospital saying goodbye to staff. We will be back every day as Dana is now considered an out-patient and is attending hourly physiotherapy sessions. Back in the hotel, we establish a routine quickly as we are encouraged by the physiotherapist to allow Dana to bear weight when we are in the hotel and work on sitting to standing. The transfers are still problematic and we take on board what works well and what we alter for next time as the transfers are between seven to eight times daily. We learn very quickly to adapt and use aids, which will make the next few weeks much easier to cope with. We get a shower seat so Dana is able to sit down. We have a footstool at the side of the bed so we are able to position ourselves for the transfer into bed. We use the space in a communal area at the back of the hotel lobby for Dana to practice sitting to standing and walking exercises, in between physiotherapy sessions at the hospital. The staff at the hotel become friends as the relationship built is one of understanding and helpfulness. We are grateful to the hotel staff and management for allowing us to be comfortable and enable us to feel it is a home away from home.

On the treadmill as part of the rehabilitation programme

The next few days sees Dana walk for the very first time on a treadmill. Not only did I think this was a piece of equipment that would be impossible for Dana to use, but also to use so close after spinal surgery. To be honest, I am a little apprehensive. Dana is so thrilled and excited to be using a treadmill and cannot wait to get started. The therapist explains to us how it starts at a very low speed and positions Dana on the treadmill. Watching on the edge of my seat, I put all my trust in the therapist as she holds Dana, supporting her weight. One thing was clear; following the operation Dana is extremely weak. It is quite alarming how much of the spasticity was 'holding Dana up' and now this had been removed how weak her muscles are. It is heartbreaking to watch Dana struggle as her legs are not supporting her fully and the therapist is supporting her hips. After just a few minutes she is crying and wanting to stop. Her face is getting redder and sweaty, but she keeps going for a few more minutes at least. What an achievement and I am so proud of Dana. The physiotherapy sessions are tough and I understand why. Seeing other children who are much further forward in their rehabilitation, it is clear this approach works and the children thrive. Younger children are encouraged through play while older children have a slightly different approach. When it comes to stretching this is universal and a strict protocol is followed by all parents regardless of the child's age.

As the days turn into weeks and the weeks turn into a month, we all become settled in a routine of daily appointments at the hospital for physiotherapy and the 'normal' routine of grocery shopping and washing. The physiotherapy sessions become more intense as Dana becomes stronger and her confidence is increasing. This is soon to pause for a day as Dana is scheduled to now have orthopaedic surgery to release both heel cords and lengthen both hamstrings. The operation itself is short and simple and following one night's stay on the ward in hospital, Dana is back resuming physiotherapy.

I am not prepared for what I am seeing. We had got Dana to the stage of walking with her frame for short distances and walking on the treadmill. The transfers were no longer needed and Dana was able to put weight on her legs long enough to step out of her wheelchair and walk a few steps with help. The day after the orthopaedic surgery when physiotherapy is due to resume again; Dana is not able to put weight on her legs. We are back to the same situation as after SDR and again we have to transfer Dana by lifting her from one point to the other. It was déjà vu all over again. I feel devastated; not only personally, but also for Dana. All the hard work that she put in is not lost. I reassure her, she will get back to that stage again, and that I know for certain. What I didn't know was how long it would take. I decide to extend our stay in the US an extra few weeks and thankfully had decided this before the orthopaedic surgery. The extended stay will allow that extra physiotherapy input, which I feel as Dana is much older than the other children, will be of great benefit and will build her strength due to the intensity of the physiotherapy programme.

Dana has to learn to walk again plain and simple. It is a case of learning how to put one foot in front of the other. Other children seem to be coping better than Dana and even at a further stage. I had to stop comparing as a lot of the other children are much younger and therefore did not have the years of disability Dana had. Dana was thirteen years of age and the average age of the younger children was four and their improvements are bigger as most had gone from a buggy to walking. Dana's improvements are much smaller and I had to start looking at the little changes, not the bigger ones. The fact that Dana is able to move her toes and her ankle would have been impossible before SDR. The fact she can lie down with her leg straight again was impossible before SDR. Seeing Dana in so much discomfort is upsetting and as a mother all you want to do is to take your child's pain away. Each day the physiotherapists are challenging Dana and encouraging her to achieve the goals set and each day I think to myself, maybe this is asking too much of Dana. Yet each day Dana achieves if not excels her goals. The personal satisfaction Dana has is clearly visible for all to see. Her smile is infectious and the therapists celebrate her achievements by cheering and clapping their hands. Dana really does have such determination in succeeding and although there are many moans and groans, so much so the therapists nickname her 'Hollywood', she never ceases to amaze me and has this inner strength.

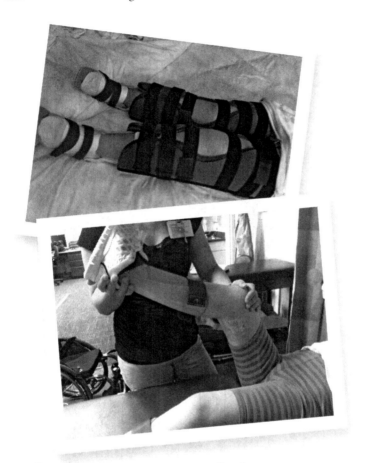

Dana wearing her nightly leg gaiters and receiving physiotherapy

Sadly the day has finally arrived for us to leave for the UK. After just under two months in the USA and experiencing the most incredible journey, Dana leaves walking confidently on her frame, without spasticity and a great future with one day walking independently at home and with a single stick in all other environments.

*On our flight back to the U.K.
Dana walked on and off the plane on
her own with sticks for the first time*

Two years of rehabilitation is required and a commitment, which both Dana and we as parents have made, even before the surgery was performed. We have already ordered the rehabilitation equipment for home as Dana is required to follow a gym programme; this excites Dana as she can be like everyone else. I'm not sure Dana fully appreciates how intense this will be as the protocol suggests a programme of five to six times per week. Once home we can incorporate a schedule, which will fit around school. For the moment though we have a list of aids and equipment, which will assist with the rehabilitation in the forthcoming months. Leg splints for day and others for night, leg gators, which Dana must wear on each leg at night. Shoe inserts for when the splints are no longer required and techniques we have picked up for stretching and exercises.

Thank you does not express how fortunate we feel for what St Louis Children's Hospital has done. They have given our daughter a future – and as parents – they have given us hope. It is a hope that we have been searching for – for many years – and a life that Dana can now live without being confined to a wheelchair. We will be forever indebted to the people who have made Dana's *Walk to the Stars* a reality.

Epilogue

IGHT months have passed and we return to St Louis for a review. Usually patients from the UK return following a year. I decide to bring our review forward as I want to ensure Dana is receiving the correct type of physiotherapy and from a personal point of view, I want to learn from the therapist different techniques to use. Dana has been in and out of splints during the past eight months, ranging from high legged to short splints and I was also looking for guidance on how many further months this will need to continue. Over the past eight months Dana has worked incredibly hard and on a combination of aqua physiotherapy, sports physiotherapy, a home gym programme and stretches twice a day. In addition to wearing day splints and night gators on both legs, I was also hoping that these had improved her range of movements. As the rehabilitation programme has been at an even pace, my feeling is the intensity can be increased, yet I am cautious because the physiotherapists in the UK have a very different approach – a much softer approach. In a way, I feel that the guidance I receive from the US physiotherapists will give me permission to increase the intensity of the programme.

Dana has also achieved the milestone that I had dreamt about; she walked from her bedroom to our bedroom on her own – an incredible sight seeing her in the doorway standing like any other person – amazing!

Rehabilitation continues at home on the treadmill

I have a very strange feeling as we land at St Louis, excited we are back and also a little nervous at the forthcoming review with both Dr Park and the orthopaedic surgeon. I have already scheduled daily physiotherapy sessions with the therapists and am very much looking forward to attending them. Walking into the hotel, it feels we have never been away, as we are greeted warmly by the staff. Ironically we have the same room booked. Taking the lift to the seventh floor, memories came flooding back of how Dana was wheeled around, how she struggled walking from the lift to the room, how she used to practice walking up and down the corridor. Opening the door to room 714, everything was the same; we even adopted the same bedroom and beds as before.

Dana on another type of rehabilitation equipment at home

Two days later we arrive at the Children's Hospital for Dana's first physiotherapy appointment. My stomach is feeling nervous as I walk in, all so familiar yet different. It's so much quieter than last time, not the usual busyness from before. As I walk through I see familiar faces greet us in their usual friendly manner. The therapist chats with us on our expectations for the next few weeks and proceeds to take some measurements of Dana's leg range. The appointment is fairly low key, which is fine as on Monday we start the hard work and have our follow-up appointment with Dr Park. The biggest milestone Dana has achieved in eight months is not using her wheelchair at all even for this journey to the USA, and I couldn't wait to hear from Dr Park how he thinks Dana has progressed, and if she is at the stage she should be. Waiting in a side room for our appointment I catch sight of Dr Park as he is finishing seeing another child, and waves hello. Soon we enter the same consultation room we were seen in before surgery. How different it feels this time, Dana walking in and not being in her wheelchair, although I am keen to know how he feels Dana has progressed, so I hang on to his every word. He confirms Dana has made excellent progress and no longer requires using the walker. She is expected to walk everywhere with sticks now, while relying only on one stick for the future. She is no longer required to wear splints. These words alone have made Dana's day, where finally she can wear the shoes she wants. We make arrangements to order the recommended shoe inserts, which fit in any shoe. Dana has the biggest smile and tells us that "she feels on top of the world". After eight months of physiotherapy 5–6 times a week together with daily stretches, we have set the foundations and Dana is on the correct path. A lot of strengthening and stretching is still required as her right side is much weaker than her left and she is as committed as ever to continue with her progress.

The good news continues later that week, as during the evaluation test where measurements are taken of Dana's range of movements, she is asked to perform set activities. Dana continues to surprise us. Her range of movements have greatly increased and far outweighed expectations, even at one year, yet we were only eight months post surgery. The orthopaedic surgeon also confirms the surgery was successful and Dana is at the stage he expects. We are thrilled at the response from the review from all parties and so pleased we returned earlier than due.

Dana and dad enjoying a celebratory ice cream

We are very excited for Dana's future, as SDR has given her a new life filled with new experiences she can now explore. The 4th

August will always be a special date and will be celebrated as the date Dana's life changed forever. St Louis Children's Hospital is very special, their consistent support and warmth in how the children and parents are cared for. There are not enough words to express our gratitude at the skilfulness of staff at the Children's Hospital. You are very special to us. Thank you.

Dana now walking with her dad

Coaching Questions

THIS part of the book will guide you by asking yourself questions specifically aimed to the chapters. They may provide some alternative thinking for you.

Chapter 1

How has changing your mindset altered your outcome?

What support systems will help you?

Chapter 2

How have you dealt with the unexpected?

What is the most meaningful action you can take?

Chapter 3

How can you gain clarity?

How does your communication help you achieve the response you want?

Chapter 4

What strategies do you use in unfamiliar situations?

What is your convincer to confirm for you things are OK?

Chapter 5

What goals can you set for yourself?

How will you know you have the right results?

Chapter 6

How can you change your mindset to achieve a positive outcome?

What resources are open to you?

Chapter 7

How do you deal with a challenging situation?

How can you gain additional support?

Chapter 8

What is the best outcome you can achieve or is there something greater?

What support is open to you?

Chapter 9

Can you think of a time you were challenged and how you dealt with this?

What changes can you make right now?

Chapter 10

Have you ever set small goals for yourself to achieve a bigger goal?

What might happen if the impossible happened, how would that look for you?

Chapter 11

What are your expectations?

What goals have you set?

Chapter 12

What difficult situations have resulted in positive outcomes for you? How will you know you have the right results?

Chapter 13

Can you think of a time you were challenged and how you dealt with this?

How can you gain additional support?

Chapter 14

What support is open to you?

How have you dealt with the unexpected?

Now I want you to imagine yourself in five years time, what can you see, feel, and hear?

References

St Louis Children's Hospital. St Louis, Missouri

http://www.stlouischildrens.org/
our-services/center-cerebral-palsy-spasticity/
about-selective-dorsal-rhizotomy-sdr

SDR at Frenchay Bristol Hospital

http://www.nbt.nhs.uk/our_services/a_-_z_of_services/n/
neurosurgery/selective_dorsal_rhizotomy.aspx

SDR At Leeds Hospital

http://www.leedsneurosurgery.com/sdr/

Support Group for Parents

http://www.support4sdr.org

Peto Institute Budapest

http://www.peto.hu/en/

About the Author

S ERA Johnston lives in Surrey with husband Glen, and their children Dana aged 14, Oliver aged 6 and their cat Marcel.

This is Sera's first book and has been a project in the thinking for years as it never seemed the right time. In 2011 following a six-month fundraising campaign to get Dana to America for an operation, Sera coordinated an appeal and raised £75,000. The operation has changed Dana's life and it now seemed the right time to write this book.

Sera is an NLP Master Practitioner and an experienced personal development coach. Sera is also an experienced trainer and facilitator, having worked in private and public organisations. Sera is passionate about developing individuals to gain a better understanding of themselves and achieve positive outcomes.

Lightning Source UK Ltd.
Milton Keynes UK
UKOW030851260912

199655UK00001B/29/P